JANE H

MAKE TRAINING
WORTH
EVERY
PENNY

ON-TARGET EVALUATION

JANE HOLCOMB·PHD

MAKE TRAINING WORTH EVERY PENNY

ON-TARGET EVALUATION

WHARTON PUBLISHING
Del Mar, CA   *1993*

Copyright ©1993 by Jane Holcomb, Ph.D

All rights reserved. No part of this book may be reproduced or utilized in any form or by any means, electronic or mechanical, including photocopying, recording or by any information storage and retrieval system, without permission in writing from the author.

Publisher's Cataloging-in-Publication Data

Holcomb, Jane, 1940-
    Make Training Worth Every Penny: On-Target Evaluation/ Jane Holcomb.

    p. cm.

    ISBN 1-56912-099-4
    1. Employees- -training of- -evaluation   1. Title
    HF 5549. 5. T7H65 1993   658. 3'12'404
    93-60065   QB193-220

Cover Design........*Dunn & Associates, Hayward, WI*
Layout Design.....*Michele Jansen, Carlsbad, CA*

Printed in the United States of America.

Dedication

To my friend and mentor, George Morrisey, who has been gently pushing me for years to write this book.

He is the published author of more than 15 books and could not understand why I would speak and teach about evaluation and not write about it. Each year he insisted this be my number one goal. Thank you George, for your encouragement and support.

Table of Contents

Introduction ix

Chapter 1. A Trainer's Dilemma 1
   Has This Happened to You? 1
   Do You Know These Managers? 3
   Dilemma #1—Whose Job Is It? 5
   Dilemma #2—What's in It for You? 6

Chapter 2. You Need Options 9
   Management Styles— Samantha, Harry or Pete 10
   What Works with Your Trainees? 26

Chapter 3. The Tool 29
   The Evaluation Chart 29
   Data Sources 33

Chapter 4. Methods for Evaluation 39
   Interviews 40
   Pre-Test/Post-Test 44
   Questionnaires and Surveys 49
   Observations 54
   Documents 59
   Simulations 65
   Action Plans 70
   Tracking Charts 75
   Gap Analysis Checklist 82

Chapter 5. The Link **89**
    Needs Assessment 91
    Program Objectives 93
    Evaluation 95

Chapter 6. The Process **101**
    Step 1—Before Training:
    Coach and Council 104
    Step 11—During Transition:
    Address Environmental Barriers 108
    Step 111—After Training:
    Reward and Reinforce 119

Chapter 7. How Managers Use the Process **127**
    Samantha and Anne 128
    Pete and Lisa 131
    Harry and David 133

Chapter 8. Closing the Loop **137**

Chapter 9. Putting It All Together **141**
    Why Evaluate Training? 141
    What Methods Can You Use? 142
    How to Choose an Instrument 143
    Three-Step Process 144
    Working with Your Managers 145
    Final Words 145

Introduction

Let me start this book with a personal story. Several years ago, before starting my company, On-Target Training, I was working with a small consulting company in Santa Monica. There were eight of us, each with a different specialty. Mine was management/supervisory development. At that time I was at USC working on my Ph.D. It was time to choose a "problem statement" for my dissertation. I was amazed at that time, as I am today, at how much money companies were willing to invest in employee training without having a clue as to whether or not it was doing the employee or the company any good. They were willing to hire expensive consultants like the ones I worked with and had no system for tracking or evaluating the results of what they were doing.

I had a hard time convincing my dissertation committee that the evaluation of employee training was a worthwhile endeavor but I was "hell-bent" on finding out how it could be done and why it was not being done. They agreed to my dissertation proposal and I spent the next several years reading everything I could find on how to evaluate training and visiting companies that were trying to evaluate their training.

Now picture this scene—It's the last time my Ph.D. committee is meeting. We are in the conference room on the eighth floor of Waite Phillips Hall. The committee is discussing my progress in the last four years. I've passed my written exam, finished my oral exams, completed my research and am now waiting for the final "yeah" or "nah" from this group. They ask me to wait in the hall. Finally the chair of the committee opens the door and signals for me to come in. The room is silent. He reaches out his hand and says, "Congratulations, Dr. Holcomb. You now have an expertise in an area that no one is interested in besides yourself."

I personally want to thank you for picking up this book. It makes me feel good to know that someone else is interested. I have developed an elegantly simple system that uses evaluation as a tool to address the real issue, which is the transfer of learning. How can we get all those good skills and ideas learned in the classroom to transfer to the work site? I will give you an academic model, methods for evaluating different kinds of training, and a process that will make the training work. The whole thing will hit you like a "lightening bolt of the obvious." This system is not a new invention. It takes things you already know and uses them in a new way. The best part is that you can make a difference using this simple system. You can make your investment in training ***worth every penny***.

Chapter 1. A Trainer's Dilemma

Has This Happened to You?

- Have you ever had bright, enthusiastic, well-motivated students who loved the program and achieved the objectives in class, go back to work eager to try new ideas and— nothing happened? Whatever was accomplished in class seemed to vanish by the time they reached the work site. What happened? Why was there no change in their performance?
- Have you ever started a training session by asking participants why they were there and what they expected to learn, only to get blank stares and shrugged shoulders? They didn't have a clue about why they were sent to training.
- Have you ever taught a class that required a new way of doing things, knowing full well, as did some of your students, that their boss would never support a change that wasn't his idea?
- Have you ever conducted a training session and realized some students were trying to learn, but were distracted by those who didn't care and were using training as a day off?

Maybe those who didn't care showed up late—or not at all? Did it dawn on you that when these negligent students returned to work they would be treated the same regarding their training experience as the ones who tried? And did you figure out that those who tried probably wouldn't try the next time?

- Would you invest your time and money in a seminar if you had no idea what you would learn or how it would help you? Yet managers send employees to training all the time without knowing the content of the program, how it will help their department, or how to reinforce what was learned.
- Have you ever collected evaluation data and then not known what to do with it except write a report that collected dust?
- Have you ever *tried* to collect evaluation data and your surveys were not returned?
- Have you ever had a manager send an employee to training to "get fixed"? The manager couldn't tell you exactly what's wrong, but training should fix it. He sent you a caterpillar and wanted a butterfly in return.
- Have you ever started a training session only to find that the tools, equipment, or software you're using are not the same as what participants use at work? This means they must unlearn what you teach and relearn on the job.
- Have you ever thought training in your organization is a series of isolated events—events for which there is no rhyme or reason? No one seems to know why training was recommended, how it relates to departmental, organizational or individual goals, or even what comes first.
- Have you ever wondered why a particular student was in a particular program? Were they sent because they were dinged on a performance appraisal and are not meeting

standards? Were they sent because they are on a fast track and being groomed for promotion? Or did they simply request the class for their own reasons?

- Have you ever been told that it's impossible to evaluate the results of training?

These are some daily training dilemmas that an appropriate evaluation system can address. Few organizations realize the value they can derive by asking the right questions based on a needs analysis and using the answers to guide future action.

This book provides a wonderfully simple evaluation system you can develop for your organization. It focuses on using evaluation as a tool to promote the transfer of learning. It does not need to be time consuming, nor does it require reams of paper work. It involves knowing what can be accomplished by evaluating training, what evaluation instruments to use, and how to use the three-step process to promote the transfer of learning. It will answer questions on evaluation like those mentioned and others you might have about your programs. The purpose of this book is to look at everything evaluation can do to make your training programs more valuable. It will help you sell and improve your programs, get managers involved and promote shared responsibility for results.

Do You Know These Managers?

Samantha is a manager who has great expectations from training. She is very demanding of herself and her employees. She is often accused of being nit-picky. She knows exactly what her employees should learn in your training session and how it should be taught. She expects to send poor performers to training and have them emerge instantly reformed, skilled, knowledgeable and productive. In short, she expects magic. If her unrealistic, superhuman expectations are not met, she blames training for not being efficient. She is also quick to point out other programs—

she's collected dozens of brochures—that make extraordinary promises to deliver everything you want to know about any subject in a half-day seminar. Samantha flashes the advertisements and expects the same types of miracles from you.

Pete is another kind of manager. He runs his department like a benevolent dictator. He believes he must retrain his people after any training session to make sure things are done his way. He has little faith in the training department's ability to understand his unique operation. He doesn't believe you are able to meet his special needs. He resents the time and money spent on training, and considers it an unnecessary expense.

Harry, on the other hand, is a manager who is like a "mother-hen" with his employees. He wants them to do well and to get the best. He also believes you can't be a prophet in your own land, and that if it's "home-grown" it can't be very good. He questions the quality of anything that in-house training provides compared to those great training gurus with big reputations and even bigger price tags. After all, if it costs more, it must be better.

Each of these managers has different objectives and expectations from training—and you are expected to satisfy them all. Can you do it? You bet! An evaluation process will help you understand each of these internal customers. By knowing their needs, wants and objectives, you can provide appropriate data, sell your programs and involve them in the evaluation process.

Evaluation can help you deal with managers like Samantha. It helps make expectations realistic and ensures that they're discussed before training occurs. It also trains Samantha to reinforce training when her employees return to work. Can Samantha get improved performance and increased productivity from training? Yes! However, the responsibility must be shared between Samantha, her trainees and the training department.

Evaluation can help you work with managers like Pete so he won't have to retrain his employees. It provides a method for Pete to give you specific data on his training requirements so you can design your programs to cover his needs. Evaluation can clearly show Pete the value of your programs to his department and to his employees.

Can you show Harry that the quality of your programs is as good as any, and that there are advantages in being "home-grown"? Of course! Evaluation can show quality and sell the additional benefit of customization. This means providing managers like Harry with additional information backed by data. But it's worth it. Once you sway Harry, *you* become the guru.

Dilemma #1—Whose Job Is It?

Who cares if students learn? Who cares if trainees are trained and use on the job what they learn in class? You and I care. I believe trainees care when their time is wasted on programs that are unplanned or inappropriate. Organizations care when their money is wasted on programs that make promises they don't deliver. Managers care when employee performance doesn't meet their goals, or when attitudes are destructive. All those who care share the responsibility for learning and for the evaluation of training; improvement requires collaboration.

Training departments can do the following:

- Conduct a needs assessment with input from managers, supervisors, trainees, customer, and others
- Design and deliver, or purchase, training programs
- Find out if participants like the programs and revise them

- Test students in class to find out if they've learned
- Provide evaluation instruments to answer other questions

Once trainees leave the classroom, trainers lose control. We need to collaborate with others in the organization to see if change has occurred on the work site.

Managers know their employees' needs and why they were recommended for training. Managers know their department goals and what training is needed for future development. Managers have the authority to address environmental barriers that can sabotage training and block improved performance. Managers need to motivate employees by rewarding and reinforcing skills learned in training. Managers need to provide evaluation data that is relevant and tells them how their employees and their departments are doing.

Employees also need to share the responsibility for their development. They can find out what training is available and request programs that provide skills they need to develop. Trainees are responsible for achieving their personal goals, which might include making commitments to action plans developed in training. Trainees need to take time to fill out surveys and questionnaires designed to improve programs provided for them.

Who's job is it? It's everyone's job. A joint effort and a joint responsibility. The training department can provide an evaluation system and lead the way.

Dilemma #2—What's In It for You?

Why bother with evaluation? If some of these benefits are important, then you need to evaluate your training:

- Employees will be properly prepared for training. They will know why they're being trained and that someone will follow-up.

- Your needs assessment will be directly related to your program objectives and evaluation methods. Evaluation results will guide your future needs assessment.
- You will provide managers with a method to give you specific information on their training and evaluation needs.
- You will be able to help managers identify environmental barriers and recommend ways to deal with them.
- Rewards and recognition will be given to employees based on progress made in training. Those who do not progress can be reinforced with something other than training.
- You will be able to demonstrate the quality and value of your programs with evaluation data.

Evaluation provides a continuous link between various training functions. The programs change, the evaluation instrument changes, but the evaluation process remains the same. An evaluation system can find out if training transferred to the job site and if not, why not? Reaction forms can help you fine tune your programs based on participant response. And evaluation can relate training to bottom-line organizational issues.

Evaluation can show you how to make your training ***worth every penny.***

Chapter 2. You Need Options

One reason evaluation efforts often fail is that those in the training department decide all of the training programs will be evaluated using a particular method. Perhaps it's a tried and true method like the pretest/posttest. It may work well for some managers and some programs, but for others it may not. It's like fitting a square peg in a round hole. For some situations, it just doesn't work. The managers don't like it and won't use it.

Evaluation is like framing a picture. Think of each program provided for employees as a different picture. You must have a frame that is appropriate, one that is chosen for a proper fit. One frame will not fit all pictures. A small, inexpensive picture does not require an elaborate frame. A more important picture calls for a bigger, more elaborate frame. The frame helps define the picture's significance. Evaluation does the same for a training program.

There are three things that will determine how you will construct your frame. Understanding these variables will give you guidance and options:

- *Your client*—what is the management style of your clients: those who will receive the evaluation data? How do they prefer to receive information?
- *Your trainees*—what works with them?
- *The program*—what are its objectives? What results are you trying to achieve?

What is the Management Style of Your Client—Samantha, Harry or Pete?

If you take all of the methods and theories on how to evaluate training and line them up on a continuum—from the most rigorous, scientific methods to the most basic—they can be divided into three categories or orientations:

```
     Most                              Most
   Rigorous                           Basic
◄─────────────────────────────────────────►
  Statistical        Business        Employee
  Orientation       Orientation     Orientation
```

It's important to understand your client's management style or orientation in order to present them with evaluation data that will be used to improve their employees' performance.

Let's take a look at each and see if you can identify your client's style and orientation toward training. They will probably be somewhere between the two extremes on this continuum. After introducing you to the orientations, there will be a short self-test to help you decide where you would fall on the continuum.

Meet Samantha—
The Research and Development Statistician

- Looks for degrees of cause and effect
- Uses scientific methods to control outside variables
- Collects statistical data
- Reports results in numbers with concern for validity and reliability

Samantha—
The Research and Development Statistician

Meet Samantha: She is an analyzer, a number cruncher, a computer jock. She thinks in facts and figures. She wants triangulation, levels of significance, and a pound of data before she will believe cause and effect. She says, "prove it to me before I believe this training program gave me these results." Managers like Samantha need numbers to make results believable, and evaluation data should be given to them in that way.

Let's use a typical scenario. Among other things, Samantha is in charge of getting the company newsletter out each month. It seems to be consistently late, which is not acceptable to her. She feels that if Anne could improve her speed on the computer and learn to use the mail merge, things would be better. Samantha decides to send Anne to a training program to improve her skills.

These are the types of questions Samantha would ask about the program:

- *Are specific goals and objectives set for the training program with quantitative methods to measure each objective?*

Example: As a result of attending this computer skills class, the participants will improve speed, demonstrate 95% competency in using the computer program and know how to use mail merge. If Samantha sends Anne to this program, they will both expect that Anne will be able to do the mail merge and work the computer with only 5% error. In addition, they will expect to see an increase in speed as she becomes more proficient.

- *Were participants given a pretest and posttest?*

Samantha would want to know if the program was aimed at the proper level for Anne. There is no point in training Anne to do something she can already do. Samantha would expect to see a significant difference in the skill Anne has after training compared with her ability going into training. If participants are not given a pretest, how can you measure the value of the training alone versus other variables that might affect Anne's performance?

- *Based on the objectives of the training, how much change can I expect to see on the job?*

Anne may perform with 100% proficiency in the classroom. However, if that skill is not transferred to the job, it will not help Samantha get her newsletter out on time. Frequently, employees attend training classes where they learn all kinds of new skills they are never able to apply on the job.

- *How much and when will the improved performance affect my productivity?*

Even Samantha realizes that the full potential of training does not occur instantly. She will have to give Anne time to improve her new skills by practicing the things she learned in training. However, she expects to see some results in a reasonable time. Perhaps the newsletter will not be on time this month, but in a month or two there should be a noticeable change.

- *Is this program teaching skills and knowledge in the most efficient way?*

Many managers have ideas about the best way to teach something; often it's the way they were taught. Samantha, like other managers, is probably inundated with advertisements from vendors selling computer training programs. Each claims wonderful results, but they have different methods for achieving them. Some are lecture and self-study orientated, some are hands-on practice in class, some work in groups with many instructors, some are small and personalized. Samantha needs to decide which program will work best for her and Anne. Which training environment will be the closest to Anne's working environment?

- ***Can the results of the training be recorded with numerical data?***

Samantha wants numbers to prove the time and money spent on Anne's training paid off. There are several ways she can collect numerical data on Anne's progress. Samantha could:

- Count the decrease in errors as Anne's skill improves
- Track progress toward on-time newsletters
- Give Anne a pretest/posttest based on speed
- Count the number of names input in the mail merge
- Determine average improvement by percent, and project future production based on continued improvement

If this is the type of information your client wants from evaluation, then they probably think like Samantha and doubt conclusions without statistical proof. For an evaluation system to work for Samantha, it must provide a method that will give her the measurable differences she is looking for.

Meet Harry—
The Employee Generalist

- Interested in providing an educational experience
- Wants to know goals of the program
- Wants information to make decisions
- Interested in unintended outcomes and participants' attitudes

Harry—
The Easy-Going, Employee Generalist

At the opposite end of the continuum is Harry, the easy-going laissez-faire type of manager. If you hand him a pile of statistical data relating to his employees' performance, he would trash it. This type of manager knows each of his people, and when he sends them to training he knows if there is an improvement in their performance. He has a gut feeling. If he is in doubt, he will "manage by walking around." He'll casually observe them, maybe stop and chat about what they thought of the training program. This is a manager who is interested in the "care and feeding" of his employees. He is concerned with their personal and individual development, and knows if he pays attention to it, their performance will improve—and so will his unit's productivity.

If your client's management style is like Harry's, he is interested in education for his employees. He wants "happy campers" and training is a means to that end. These are qualitative questions that do not produce numbers, but give information on the quality of the training and its effect on employees.

Let's look at Harry working with one of his employees. David is one of his best and most consistent salesmen. However, lately his record shows he's in a slump. Although Harry keeps an eye on David, he tries not to put more pressure on him by grilling him about his recent poor showing. Harry is delighted when David approaches him to address the problem. Harry suggests a sales training course he heard about. He has heard from his colleagues, who are sales managers in other companies, that this program is very good. It motivates people who are in a slump and is designed for experienced salesmen who want to focus on cross-selling to current clients. David is willing to try anything.

These are the type of questions Harry would ask about a program for David:

- *What is the nature of the program?*

Is it well organized, entertaining? Does it have a great instructor who is enthusiastic and can motivate David? Harry knows that David has sales skills. Right now he needs to be inspired and motivated to do what he knows how to do. A few new ideas would be nice, but mostly David needs to be recharged. Harry has heard this instructor can do just that; he is a dynamo and participants come out feeling like they can walk on water.

- *Does the program allow participants to discuss individual concerns and problems?*

Harry is not sure what is causing David's slump. He has tried a few of his old tricks to get the ball rolling, but nothing has helped. Perhaps in a new environment, with peers who are strangers and non-threatening, he can reveal and work out whatever is bothering him. Harry feels this week-long sales class will give David some time to think and talk to others who have perhaps had the same problem he's having. Harry could call the instructor to find out how the class is run and if there will be opportunities like that.

- *What are the unintended outcomes of this program?*

Perhaps they are more significant than the program objectives. Unintended outcomes are beyond the stated objectives of the course. One example is sending people to a sales training program to improve sales, and discovering the program also builds self-confidence and gives participants insight into their personalities and ways of dealing with others. It is sending employees to a sales training program to increase their bottom-line, and finding that they built a network of resource people from other companies who became friends as well as information sources. It is sending your salesmen to learn how to cross-sell, and finding that the program also encouraged team building and improved communication and cooperation among them. These outcomes may be more important to the trainee and the company than the program's stated objectives.

Unintended outcomes are generally overlooked as a way of evaluating training and almost never included in the evaluation process. It would take a manager like Harry, who has personal concern for his employees, to see the intrinsic value in the unintended outcomes.

- *What are the goals and objectives of the program and do they meet my employees' needs?*

Harry knows his employees. He knows any old basic sales training course would not be appropriate for an experienced salesman like David. In fact, it might be an insult. Harry has chosen this class carefully with David's particular needs in mind. David needs motivation, he needs his confidence rebuilt, he needs to discuss his sales slump with other professional salesmen. The objective of this class is not to teach Sales 101. If it were, it would not be appropriate for David. He is fortunate to have a manager like Harry who is able and willing to understand his needs before recommending training.

- *Will my employee like this workshop?*

The most basic way to evaluate training is to find out if the participants liked it. Some managers do not care whether or not their employees liked training. If they liked it, but it made no change in their performance, was it a worthwhile investment? On the other hand, if they didn't like the class, are they likely to use any of the ideas presented? Harry feels they must like it to learn it, internalize the ideas, and use them. Harry is the type of manager who appreciates this concept and one of his primary questions would be, "Will David like this class?" When discussing the possibility of this class with David, if Harry felt there was some reason David would not want to attend, Harry would drop the idea. Harry believes that to learn anything, an employee must want to learn. If personal matters could interfere, then it's probably not a good investment of David's time or company money.

If your client's management style is like Harry's, these are the type of questions he would ask about his employees' training. These are qualitative questions that do not produce numbers, but give information on the quality of the training and the effect it will have on his employees. A main concern for managers like Harry is the quality of life for his employees and the organization as a whole. Training that improves performance also improves the quality of life. Isn't everyone happier when they perform well?

Meet Pete—
The Business Practitioner

- Interested in participant's reaction
- Wants knowledge, skill, and attitude development
- Seeks changes in on-the-job behavior
- Looks for bottom-line business results

Pete—
The Business Practitioner

Meet Pete, the practical business-oriented manager. He is someone who grew up with the company, advanced through the ranks. The company and its success are important to him. He knows the production process better than anyone. He also knows the company's history and the skeletons hidden in the closets. He is pragmatic, and earned his college degree on company time and money. His education was to help him do his job better. He would evaluate training by asking these four questions:

1. *Did they like it?*

How did the trainees feel about the program, the instructor and the whole learning experience?

2. *Did they learn it?*

Were the objectives of the program achieved? Did the trainees know more after the program than before?

3. *Can they use it?*

Are the ideas, skills, attitudes relevant to the trainees and transferrable to their jobs?

4. *So what—how does it affect my bottom-line?*

Even if the answers to the first three questions are "yes," does it make a difference to the organization as a whole?

Pete works with people in a very direct manner. Looking for better quality and more efficient ways to run his department, he is always aware of production goals. His eye is not on numbers, like Samantha's, nor on the individual, like Harry's. His eye is on the task, on the job at hand. He needs people and numbers to run the business.

Let's look at another scenario. Pete has a problem. The first line supervisor who reports to Pete has been disappointing him lately. The quality of his work has gone down and lately he has been frequently absent. Pete suspects he is looking for a position with another company and is planning on replacing him. Pete is considering sending one of his employees, Lisa, to training. Lisa has been working in Pete's department for two years. She is young, but is dependable and willing to learn. Without making promises, he wants to encourage Lisa to learn new skills. He would like to be able to recommend her for promotion if the opportunity arises. Pete suggests that Lisa attend an in-house training program for supervisors that teaches the internal procedures for reconditioning and fixing delicate machines. This means more work for Lisa, but she seems ready to handle the added responsibility and responds to the idea with enthusiasm.

These are the type of questions Pete would ask about Lisa's training. Donald Kirkpatrick, originator of the following commonly accepted evaluation method, identifies them as levels I - IV.

- *Level I—What are Lisa's reactions to the program?*

Will she enjoy this kind of work? What was her reaction to the training itself? What is her reaction to the class? Did she like it? If she does not enjoy the task, the way it was taught, the class itself, then it's not likely that she will learn much from it. So Pete would first want to know if Lisa liked it. What were her reactions when the class was finished?

- *Level II—Pete's second question is did she learn it?*

Was Lisa able to learn the skills that were being taught and did she understand them? After attending the class, does Lisa understand the procedures for fixing machinery and is she able to do it correctly? Did she learn how to do what the session and the instructor intended? Level II of evaluation is done in the classroom. The instructor would want to test Lisa to make sure she is competent and confident about using her new skills before she leaves the classroom.

- *Level III—Can Lisa actually use the new skills on the job?*

There are many things that prevent trainees from using their skills. Pete's concern is whether Lisa can transfer what she has learned in class to the job. The problems are not as cut and dried as they are in class. It often requires judgment, and there is no instructor or other students to ask. How does Lisa do in those cases? Did the training program teach her how to adapt her new skills to her job, to the unique problems and situations she finds? This is an extremely important point for Pete. The fact that she liked the class and can do it in class has little value to him if she can't transfer that skill to the work site. Kirkpatrick's Level III of evaluation is the ability to use it. This level is seldom evaluated in organizations. It requires follow-up after the student leaves the classroom. Pete is the type of manager who would follow-up with Lisa. However, even a well-meaning manager like Pete needs some help. He needs to have some tools or guidelines. Pete wants to see a change in Lisa's knowledge and skill as a result of sending her to the training program.

- *Level IV—How does this training affect my bottom-line?*

Results can be measured in many ways. Are trainees more productive? Are employees communicating better, is the manager saving time by not resolving conflicts? Has customer service improved and have customer complaints decreased? Are supervisors doing a better job and, therefore, do we have lower turnover and fewer grievances?

In this particular class, the bottom-line for Pete would be to see Lisa independently fix machines when her supervisor was out, since eventually he would like to have her take over this function. This would increase productivity in Pete's department and have a positive effect on his bottom-line. The training program would meet Pete's need by solving a problem for him and helping him plan for future needs.

These three managers want different information about their employees' training. The same evaluation method would not satisfy Samantha, Harry and Pete. Their management style contributes to the type of questions they ask about their employees' training. It indicates the manner in which they like to receive information and the way they relate to their employees. Do you know some managers and supervisors in your organization who are like Samantha, Harry and Pete?

This self-test is a job aid to help you and your clients figure out what to look for when evaluating training. One method will not work for all situations. Sometimes you need to think like Samantha and sometimes like Harry. Where does your client fall on the continuum between rigorous and basic? Which group has the most checks?

When I Evaluate Training, I Look for the Following

Please check all that apply to you.

Group 1
- ☐ Were specific goals set with quantitative measures?
- ☐ How much was learned in the program?
- ☐ How much does the behavior change affect productivity?
- ☐ Is this program teaching the right things in the right way, or is there a better way?
- ☐ Can the results be supported with numerical data?

Group 2
- ☐ How do the participants feel about the program and what is their reaction to it?
- ☐ Are the goals and objectives of the program attained in the training sessions?
- ☐ What are the unintended outcomes of the program? (Increased confidence, improved self-image, team building, etc.)
- ☐ Is this program a means to the desired end?
- ☐ Is this program well managed and well planned?

Group 3
- ☐ How does the program help the department and the organization?
- ☐ How does it affect profit and loss, cost and benefit?
- ☐ Is the training producing more competent employees?
- ☐ How can training improve the use of our human resources?
- ☐ What have employees learned, and can they apply it on the job?

If most of your answers were in—	Your dominant orientation is—
Group 1	Statistician *(Samantha)*
Group 2	Generalist *(Harry)*
Group 3	Practitioner *(Pete)*

What Works with Your Trainees?

Evaluation of training should be a benefit to your trainees. It gives them an opportunity to show their ability to improve their performance. It will be a win-win situation if you collaborate with the trainees, as well as their manager, when choosing a method for evaluation. A good method for some may not be good for others. A few examples:

- Some employees do very well on written tests, which give them an opportunity to show what they know. Other employees who do equally well on the job may panic when it comes to a test. This is especially true of employees who speak English as a second language. Their numbers are growing, and our ways of evaluating their skills must allow other methods for them to show what they can do.
- Some employees perform well when they are being observed. Sometimes that is the *only* time they perform well. Other employees may freeze or act very unnatural when being observed. They do well on their own, but this method of evaluation is a hindrance for them. I remember being able to type pretty well in high school when I was *at home*. But in class, with the teacher looking over my shoulder, my fingers would freeze.
- Some employees are slow learners. It's not that they can't learn, it just takes them a little more time, and your evaluation of their training must take this into account.
- Keeping score for teams and individuals motivates many employees who enjoy the competition and camaraderie of working toward goals. Managers who grew up playing on teams like to evaluate with score cards. However, there are always those with the low scores. They are not only deflated by this method: It might even discourage them from trying. Those who give up easily, or who must be the best but are not, will not do well with this type of evaluation.

- Interviews are a common way to evaluate training. There are some employees who can demonstrate their new knowledge and goals and enjoy talking about it. In fact, the interview reinforces their learning. Other employees use a lot of hot air; they are experts at creating verbal smoke screens. Interviewing them is a waste of your time and theirs.
- Some employees enjoy having you closely track training progress and like compliments from you on each small improvement. Others consider that patronizing and resent your hovering over them.

What are your trainees like? What is the best way to work with them? Looking at what motivates your trainees will help you decide how to evaluate their training.

Remember, the goal of evaluation is to get learning to transfer from the classroom to the work site to improve performance and productivity. You don't want your method of evaluation to sabotage that goal. That is why one method will not suit each situation. You need to collaborate with trainees to find out what will work best to motivate them to use their new skills on the job.

What Are the Program Objectives?

The content and objectives of the programs employees attend are very different. Think of some of the various types of programs your company provides and employees request. What does each program intend to teach the participants? What are the learning and behavioral objectives? The content of the class will vary based on program objectives. To support and reinforce results, managers need to know what your trainees will be learning. The objectives of the program will help determine the nature of the evaluation method. Consider the content and objectives of a computer training program for new employees versus a team building program for senior management. The same method of evaluation would not be appropriate for programs with such diverse objectives.

Some organizations have catalogues they produce each year with hundreds of training programs available to employees. Some allow employees to attend as many programs as they want. Some organizations reimburse any accredited college level course. Some require 40-50 hours of annual training per employee. With such variety, you could not possibly evaluate each program using the same method.

The point is that you need options. One method of evaluation is not appropriate for all situations. It must be based on management style, what works with your trainees, and the content of the program.

That brings us back to the picture frame. You must create a frame that will fit each picture, each situation you deal with. One frame won't fit all pictures. If you think of your program as the picture, then you can customize the frame to fit.

Chapter 3. The Tool

The Evaluation Chart

The *tool*, the evaluation chart, is used as a job aid to help you construct your picture frame. It consists of data sources that include people who can tell you about your training. The data sources are listed across the top of the On-Target Evaluation Chart. On the side are various methods you can use to evaluate the training program. By combining a data source and a method, you come up with a variety of ways to build your picture frame.

You have options. There are several combinations of sources and methods that would be appropriate for most situations. Your choice depends on your client's management style, what works with your trainees, and the objectives of the program. The evaluation chart is your tool to determine how you will evaluate the training.

I'll discuss how to use the evaluation chart again when we talk about the transfer process. Remember, evaluation is a tool to address the real issue, which is transfer of learning. How do we get that good stuff learned in the classroom out to the work site?

First, use the chart to ask if there will be a difference in performance or productivity as a result of training. If performance and productivity can be measured, then training can be measured. If it cannot, perhaps you should question the value of the training program. Every program that you provide should have objectives and results.

Second, collaborate with your clients, the trainees' managers, to determine their management style. How do they want data and results reported? This will lead to which method should be used for collecting data.

Third, choose the best source for collecting data. Who can give you the information you need? Next, discuss the plan with potential trainees. You can now select a method for evaluation. Place a date on the chart for the appropriate time to conduct the evaluation. The training department can now design an evaluation instrument that is appropriate for each program provided for employees.

On-Target Evaluation

Name: _____

Training Class: _____ Date: _____

Name of Supervisor: _____

Evaluation:

Methods	Sources					
	Trainee	Boss	Peers	Employees	Customers	Others
Interviews						
Pretest/Posttest						
Questionnaire/Survey						
Observation						
Documents						
Simulations						
Action Plans						
Tracking Charts						
Checklist						
Others						

Comments: _____
_____
_____
_____

Together you can determine an appropriate method of evaluation. In addition, you can agree on a follow-up date.

- Some managers want to keep all of the evaluation charts indicating programs their employees have attended. It helps them keep track of which employees have attended each program.
- Some managers keep them in each employee's file and make a note in their own time-management book about the follow-up data.
- Some managers ask employees to be responsible for evaluation and a follow-up date, especially if the employees will be eager to demonstrate their new skills. This frequently occurs when the completion of training makes them eligible for a possible promotion.
- Some managers want the training department to be in charge of evaluation data and keep records for them.

Again, there is no one right way. The evaluation chart is a job aid, a tool to help work with your managers to develop the best method for evaluation.

After employees return from training, the evaluation chart is used again. This time to identify any problems. Are the trainees doing what the manager expected as a result of training? If so, great! Let them go, and compliment their success and yours. If not, you can determine through evaluation what is preventing them from using their new skills or ideas. This will be discussed further in Chapter 6 under Environmental Barriers.

Use the evaluation chart to remind managers to reinforce and reward those who become better as a result of training. You can use it as a tool to identify individuals who have changed, and reward their progress. I'll discuss proper rewards in Chapter 6. Just a reminder—if a gain is to be maintained it must be reinforced and rewarded. The evaluation chart can help you identify and keep track of those who need reinforcement and those who deserve rewards.

You can use the evaluation chart to enhance your needs assessment. Managers can gather specific information about training so the training department can meet their training needs.

This is especially relevant for in-house programs where you are there to provide for organizational and department needs. Many times the training department can only second-guess what managers want because of insufficient information from their needs assessment. Many times managers are not sure of what they want until they see what they get.

The evaluation chart can help you:

- Collect clear and specific data from those in charge of providing training for their employees
- Identify problems and discover environmental barriers that interfere with achieving results
- Reward and reinforce those who have made progress as a result of training
- Give you an opportunity to collaborate with managers and employees to figure out the best method to evaluate progress and development.

The evaluation chart is a tool, a job aid, to help you ask the right questions.

Data Sources

Let's take a closer look at the data sources. Surprisingly, there are only a handful of people you can go to for information on training results. Who can best give you that information? Each program presents a different situation. If a program was developed in response to a problem, then your source will be obvious. For instance, if a customer service program was started as a result of customer complaints, then an important data source would be the customers—to see if complaints decreased. If that same customer service program was started because of requests from supervisors to train new employees, then your data source might be the requesting supervisors—to see if new employees are adequately trained. I once created a customer service program in response to requests from service agents. They did not feel comfortable with new insurance forms. The proper data source for that customer service program were the trainees, those who needed to use the new forms. Your first clue in choosing a data source is to ask why this program was created.

With a little common sense you'll identify the best person for the information you want. Occasionally, your ideal or first choice is not available or impractical to reach. Remember, there is no one right way to evaluate training. There are several sources and several methods available. Try Plan B! What other source could you tap for the information you want? Most of the time you will find several possible options and your problem will be which one to choose.

For some managers who think like Samantha, one will not be enough. They will want two or three data sources to prove to themselves and others that the training really worked, that the training was in fact responsible for certain changes.

Here are the recommended data sources and examples of when you might use them:

Trainee. A self-evaluation is done by going directly to the trainees for their perception of what was accomplished in training.

> *Example*: Take our scenario of David, who is in a sales slump. His sales are down and his confidence is low. His boss hears of a highly-touted motivational sales trainer

who will be delivering a one-week seminar. The boss recommends the program and the employee is willing to try anything. After the program, the most appropriate data source to go to would be David. You'd want to find out if he thought it helped him out of his slump and determine what new ideas he got from the seminar.

Supervisor. This refers to the trainee's immediate supervisor, not one several levels up. The person who observes the trainee on the job day in and day out. This may be a district manager, a first-line supervisor, or a department head. It is the trainee's supervisor who is in the best position to tell if there is a change on the job as a result of training. This person frequently does the performance appraisal or contributes to it.

Example: John is "dinged" on his performance appraisal for his inability to delegate work. There is a module offered in a basic supervisory course that deals with delegation. It is an in-house program and open to all employees. The supervisor strongly recommends that John attend the course. After the program, the best source of data on whether or not it helped is likely to be the supervisor who detected the problem and recommended training. That would be the logical source to determine if John had improved his ability to delegate. A second source might be John's employees, those to whom he delegates. They could also give information as to whether John has improved as a result of training.

Peers. These include those who are on the same organizational level and working side by side with a trainee.

Example: Susan is about to attend a popular program on team-building and communication skills. It uses a personality profile index. It asks peers, as well as others, to rate each trainee on a number of communication skills. The information will be fed back to Susan anonymously during training. Skills are identified for her to work on. The data is collected again some time later to see if she has improved. Collecting data from peers, in this case systematically and anonymously, is a good source to indicate the effect of training. It will tell you how Susan is perceived by her peers before and after training as indicated on the profile.

Employees. Those people who work for the person in training are another good source. They could be one level or several levels below the trainee. Those being managed and supervised are well positioned to evaluate managers and supervisors.

Example: Arlene worked at a large insurance company. A lot of time and effort was put into developing a performance appraisal training program for all new managers. It covered how to use the performance appraisal forms, how to motivate employees, how to conduct the interview, and how to use the performance appraisal system for its original intent—to improve performance. Her employees, those who are being appraised, determined the ability of a manager to conduct a good, constructive performance appraisal. They were asked to evaluate Arlene's ability to help them set goals, stay on track, and improve performance.

Customers. These can be external or internal. Many training programs are instigated in response to customer concerns. The customer frequently is the best source of information to see if the service has improved as a result of training.

Example: A rent-a-car company has had some complaints about the attitude of the front-line people behind the counter. The complaints are directed at the service agents in general, not at specific individuals. They say the agents seem inattentive, preoccupied, and disinterested in the customers. The company hired an outside vendor to provide customer service workshops. All of the service agents attended. After the workshops, two methods were used to evaluate the results. First, written complaints were reviewed to see if customer complaints had decreased. In addition, customers were randomly interviewed when they left the counter to see if their perception of the agents' attitude had improved.

Others. There are occasionally other sources of information, but they aren't as common as the five listed. The trainer in the classroom could be a data source on skills demonstrated in a controlled environment. An outside consultant is occasionally hired for the purpose of evaluation. Supermarkets and others hire secret shoppers. There are many other possibilities for specific programs such as the example that follows.

> *Example*: Joan was formerly in charge of the secretarial pool at a large aerospace company. She said many of their managers were sent to a class on business-writing skills. Even after training, some of them were terrible writers and turned in "chicken scratches and garbage" to the secretarial pool. However, by the time the secretaries edited, corrected, and tweaked it, the end result was pretty good. The only ones who knew if the training program helped were the secretaries who saw the work before they fixed it. They are likely to be the best data source for this particular program.

To summarize data sources, it would be safe to say that 80% of the time you will use one of the five data sources listed on the On-Target Evaluation Chart. Occasionally you will come up with another source. Remember, there is no one right way. I want to encourage you to be creative and think of your particular program, trainee, and client's management style before you select a data source. Ask yourself, "Why was this program originated and who can tell me if it worked?"

Chapter 4. Methods for Evaluation

Your tool, the On-Target Evaluation Chart, lists on the top data sources we described in the previous chapter. These sources are limited to a handful. Methods, on the other hand, have no limit. There are nine examples listed. If you learn to use these methods, most of your evaluation needs will be covered. Other methods are also useful; this list could be longer. In addition to these, you may have a workable method of your own, or a new method may be invented tomorrow.

This chapter briefly describes each method. It discuses the pros and cons of each method and typical data sources. There will be an example of how to use the method and a sample form constructed for that example.

Interviews

Interviews can be formal and structured or a very informal "How did it go?" discussion. The objective is to ask various people about the specific training program. An interview is usually conducted on a one-to-one basis. Focus groups are interviews with small groups. You need to take notes during the interview to have information you can refer to later. A formal, structured interview uses a form and each person is asked exactly the same questions. An informal interview invites detours and open discussion.

Advantages of the Interview

- You can probe for information. When someone makes a comment, it may lead to another question. The information you get from the unplanned questions may be more valuable than your original question. Interviews are more candid than other methods. You can get very personal opinions and information in an interview. People are willing to talk about almost anything if you show genuine concern and interest in their answers.

- Information is collected from those interviewed. Other instruments can get lost or are never returned. If you need 20 responses, you might send out 100 surveys. The interview provides instant and definite feedback. You do not have to wait for your information to rise to the top of someone's in-basket. Your top priority is often not theirs. You actually have data from those you choose to interview.

- The interviewee is free to volunteer information. One thing leads to another; the most interesting conversations are never planned. You enter with some questions and an agenda. If you use these to get the conversation started, the interviewees will join in, and their agendas may be more interesting than yours. After all, they have access to a grapevine that may never reach you. The person you are interviewing has an opportunity to present ideas and opinions that may be unexpected.

- The interview permits you to select whom you want information from. Perhaps you value the opinions of some more than others. It's okay. Some people may simply supply more reliable information—or you happen to respect their opinions more than those of others. After working with people, there are those you learn to trust and those whose colored versions of what is happening is only vaguely related to the real world.
- Structured interviews can provide quantitative data. Rating scales are often used. The questions would sound like this, "On a scale of one to five, how would you rate our customer service?"

Disadvantages of the Interview

- Interviews are time-consuming and generally done on a one-to-one basis, which also makes them costly. If time is money, it is expensive to interview lots of people. However, if you want specific information, it's worth the effort. The cost of inappropriate training is considerably more expensive than the time it takes to interview.
- Structured interviews need to be planned and information documented. To provide quantitative data from interviews, the same questions must be asked of each person. In fact, the question should be asked in the same way, same tone of voice, etc. In a structured interview, you do not answer questions or engage in conversation of any sort. You simply repeat the questions so that each person has an equal opportunity to interpret and respond. Their responses can then be analyzed and quantified.

Sources for the Interview

- Interviews are appropriate with all sources. Almost anyone can be interviewed, depending on the information needed.

        Trainees   Employees

        Supervisors   Customers

        Peers   Others

Interview Examples

A group of salespeople from a large real estate company was trained on how to change its hard-line selling style to a more consultive method. The group was trained to learn more about its clients' needs versus wants, and to serve as advisors so the client, the company and the salesperson would end up in a win-win situation. The training was conceived as a result of too many deals falling out of escrow because aggressive realtors were selling buyers properties that were over their budgets. The company wanted to change its philosophy to a more customer-oriented service image. After training, the sales managers conducted interviews to see if each of the salespeople understood the new philosophy and the consulting process.

The office manager also conducted interviews with new clients to see if salespeople were using their new skills on the job.

The worksheet on the following page was designed for the sales manager to use when a trainee returned from the seminar. The questions are based on the training program's objectives.

Real Estate Consulting Skills

Name: _____   Date: _____

What did you learn about Consultive Selling?

- _____
- _____

What are some key questions you need to ask clients?

- _____
- _____

What ideas can you offer on creative financing that could help your client?

- _____
- _____

How would you advise clients who really cannot afford the property they want?

- _____
- _____

Pretest/Posttest

The pretest/posttest, is one of the most common and reliable ways to evaluate training. In its basic form, you simply find out what trainees know or can do before training. When they finish training, they should know more and be able to perform better. A pretest/posttest is generally a written set of questions to determine knowledge. A similar set of questions is given before and after, to see if the trainee has learned anything. A pretest/posttest can also be applied to behavior and skills, and does not need to be written. A manager could test behavior before training by observing performance on the job. Counting mistakes, complaints, widgets produced before training and counting change after is a pretest/posttest. The same method used to identify a problem before training would be used after. Training is provided to improve the performance and a posttest is used after training to evaluate the improvement. The difference in employee's skills, knowledge or attitudes before and after is a pretest/posttest.

Advantages of Pretest/Posttest

- The pretest helps determine if training is needed. Occasionally a pretest is given only to find out that the employees know what is needed to perform the job. Perhaps a lack of motivation or some other barrier is preventing them from doing what they know how to do. If that's the case, the pretest would indicate that training is not the proper solution.
- The pretest can help isolate exactly what employees know and need to know. That way you can make sure the training program you provide will meet their needs. There are many programs under a generic title that have different objectives. "Communication skills" can mean many things. If someone is sent to communication skills training to improve his writing skills, be sure this program

doesn't teach public speaking. The pretest can help determine exactly what an individual needs so that you can provide a program to match that need.

- The pretest can make employees aware of what they need to learn. Employees often feel they are doing just fine and even know it all. A pretest can point out what they don't know and motivate them to learn some new things in training.

- Pretests are often given in training sessions on a routine basis. They test what participants know entering the class. The same or similar test is given at the program's conclusion to see if the students learned the information. Training people do this to improve their class and teaching skills. If students are not accomplishing certain objectives, then we try a new approach. Managers generally do not ask for this data and trainers do not send it to them. However, pretest/posttest information could help managers and HRD work together to improve employee performance.

- The pretest/posttest method can be considered reliable, verifiable, scientific data if some precautions are taken. This is a method that a manager like Samantha relies on. Only the training program should account for the change. Other variables such as increased staff, downsizing, economic conditions, new machinery, new management, etc., can affect employee performance and productivity. If variables are controlled, pretest/posttest provides reliable, verifiable, statistical data.

- You can give pretest/posttests at various time intervals. The test can be given directly after training, several weeks later, or several months later to determine if what was learned in training was maintained over a long period.

- You can use the results of the pretest/posttest to get information on many things. You can compare groups of students. You can compare programs, instructors, teaching methods or technical ways of presenting information. You can use it to measure attitudes, skills, knowledge—almost anything.

Disadvantages of the Pretest/Posttest

- The pretest/posttest must be planned and developed before training, based on the program objectives. If you just evaluate what people know after training, then you can't say that the training was responsible. Perhaps they knew what was taught before they went into the program.
- The experts don't agree on how pretest/posttest should be done. The bad news is that there are no clear guidelines that everyone agrees on. The good news is that your way is as good as any. If you get the information you need, then use whatever method works for you.
- Some people are not good at taking tests. They simply freeze—get mental blocks. These same people might perform well on the job or do fine with another type of evaluation method.
- Pretests and posttests are generally written. Many workers for whom English is a second language do not understand the words on the test. There are many people from foreign countries who know how to drive but can't pass the written exam if it is given in English.

Sources for the Pretest/Posttest

Unlike the interview, where almost anyone could be interviewed in certain situations, there is only one data source for the pretest/posttest. The only person who can be tested is the employee who participated in the program. The pretest/posttest is designed for the trainee.

Pretest/Posttest Example

Managers in a large public utility noticed that reports written by staff people had to be rewritten several times. The reports were too long and didn't include relevant information. Most of them were too wordy and never got to the point. The situation was wasting managers' time and aggravating the staffers who thought their reports were acceptable. An outside consultant was hired to improve writing skills. He needed to teach staff people to be concise but include pertinent information. Samples of their reports were collected to determine their length and whether or not they included relevant data.

The pretest confirmed that a business-writing program was needed; it also isolated those who needed to attend and those who did not. The objectives of the class were to get people to cut down the length of their documents by editing ferociously and checking to include *who, what, where, when* and *why*. After the class, a new batch of reports were reviewed by the managers. They found a great improvement and considered the training program successful. Plans were made to review the reports again at a later date to determine if the improvement was maintained. The evaluation form on the following page was used for this program.

Business Writing Workshop

Objective: Brief memos, letters, & reports

# of Pages: Before   After   %

Memos   _____   _____   _____
Letters   _____   _____   _____
Reports   _____   _____   _____

(Find the difference before and after, divide by original to get % of change.)

Objective: Overcoming "Page Fright"

Did the Business-Writing Workshop make you more confident by making it easier to get started?

        Yes ____   No ____

How do you get started with a writing project?

_____
_____
_____
_____

Objective: Complete documents—*who, what, where, when, why.*

Review documents produced after training. Do they contain the above information or all important information?

#1. ____ Yes   ____ No   #4. ____ Yes   ____ No
#2. ____ Yes   ____ No   #5. ____ Yes   ____ No
#3. ____ Yes   ____ No   #6. ____ Yes   ____ No

Result: ____ % complete (count yes answers, divide by total)

Is this result satisfactory?   ___ Yes   ___ No

Questionnaires and Surveys

At some time, every one of you has filled out a questionnaire or survey that provided information for someone to evaluate a product, service or program. The most familiar in the training field are the reaction forms that follow most training programs. They ask if you liked the program, how you would rate it on a scale of one to ten, etc. A questionnaire or survey can be a few questions on a card—as you see in hotels for customer satisfaction information, or it can be several pages—as in a government census report. There is probably more variety to surveys and questionnaires than other evaluation forms. Those filling them out often do not know they are providing evaluation data for someone.

Advantages of Questionnaires and Surveys

- They are non-threatening. We do them so often that we don't think of them as a test. It's perceived as merely a way to collect "my" opinion to improve a product or a service. Most people like to think their opinions count.

- Surveys and questionnaires come in various forms. They can have open-ended questions where comments are requested. This gives people freedom to say whatever they choose about the program. Multiple choice limits the answers to the choices listed. Rating scales ask for opinions that provide numerical data. Some have true/false or yes/no choices. The variety available is an advantage to creating a questionnaire or survey to suit your needs.

- You can collect vast amounts of information with questionnaires or surveys by tabulating the results on a computer. The presidential elections are a type of questionnaire or survey to see who we "like" best.

- Survey information can be anonymous. This gives people the freedom to answer honestly without fear of repercussion. When people have a negative comment, they will often not complain. An anonymous survey will allow them to voice their feelings.
- Surveys can be qualitative, quantitative or both. They can collect opinions on how people perceive improvement in a skill. When enough opinions are collected, results can be quantified with statistics.

Disadvantages of Surveys and Questionnaires

- You never really know who filled them out unless they are done in front of you. For example, surveys can be sent out to managers to get their opinions or attitudes on something. The secretary fills it out to save the manager time. The opinions collected are not those of managers, but from whomever happened to respond.
- Careful thought needs to be given to how questions are worded. Words are perceived differently by each of us. The words *often, frequently, sometimes,* and *rarely,* mean different things to different people. For example, a group of managers was asked to assign a number to the statement, "this employee is often late to work." The numbers quoted for "often" ranged from six times a month to thirty times a month.
- Surveys and questionnaires are often sent out, but not returned. Unless there is a way to track your survey and follow-up, many will never come back. People do not consider surveys or questionnaires a priority, especially if they are long, time-consuming and anonymous.
- The information received on the surveys and questionnaires is limited to the questions asked. Unlike an interview where you can probe for information, you only get what you ask for in a questionnaire. In addition, if a question is not clear, the person cannot ask for clarification; so, the answer is based on interpretation.

- The results from surveys and questionnaires are often skewed or stated in ways that are misleading. When you hear of *every* new automobile being rated as number one, you wonder what question was asked on the survey.

Sources for Questionnaires and Surveys

Almost any source can be used. You can send surveys or questionnaires to the same sources you would interview. The difference is in the amount and type of response.

Surveys are most common when large amounts of data are needed—such as customer satisfaction.

Questionnaire and Survey Examples

A chain of retirement homes was interested in improving its service to residents as the result of written complaints presented to the administrator. A survey was taken on resident satisfaction, asking several questions regarding food service, housekeeping, and other issues that resulted from the complaints.

The survey found residents were most unhappy with the food, the service in the dining rooms, and the dining room policy. They also identified issues regarding the reception service at night and concern for their safety. The original Residents' Satisfaction Survey led to a task force of residents that was asked to expand the survey and find specific improvements that would increase satisfaction.

As a result, the administrator hired an outside training company to review the survey information and provide a training program that would address specific issues. Managers and employees were trained on customer service, communication skills, and job skills.

After the training was completed, another resident satisfaction survey was conducted to see if the satisfaction level had increased. It was decided that a similar survey would be conducted annually. The cost of the survey paid off in resident involvement and their participation in solving problems. The evaluation form on the following page is a sample of the type of questions used on the survey.

Resident Satisfaction Survey

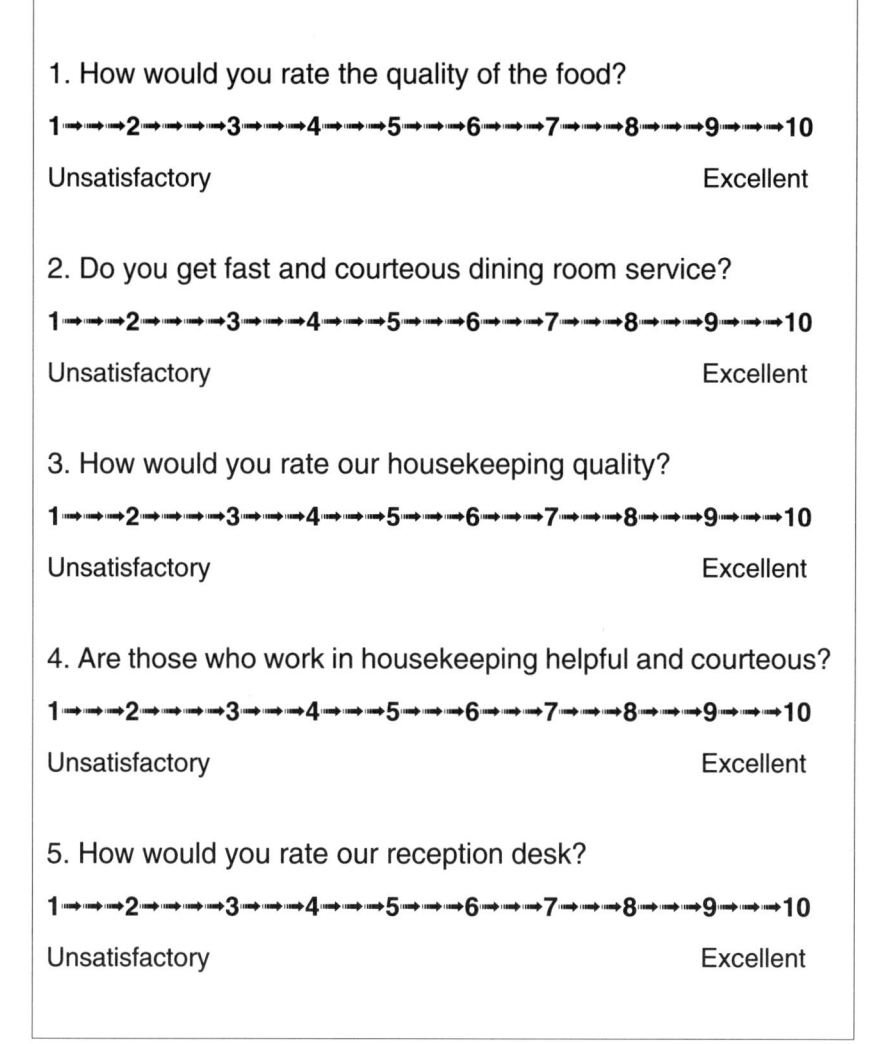

1. How would you rate the quality of the food?

1➡➡2➡➡➡3➡➡➡4➡➡➡5➡➡➡6➡➡➡7➡➡➡8➡➡➡9➡➡➡10

Unsatisfactory   Excellent

2. Do you get fast and courteous dining room service?

1➡➡2➡➡➡3➡➡➡4➡➡➡5➡➡➡6➡➡➡7➡➡➡8➡➡➡9➡➡➡10

Unsatisfactory   Excellent

3. How would you rate our housekeeping quality?

1➡➡2➡➡➡3➡➡➡4➡➡➡5➡➡➡6➡➡➡7➡➡➡8➡➡➡9➡➡➡10

Unsatisfactory   Excellent

4. Are those who work in housekeeping helpful and courteous?

1➡➡2➡➡➡3➡➡➡4➡➡➡5➡➡➡6➡➡➡7➡➡➡8➡➡➡9➡➡➡10

Unsatisfactory   Excellent

5. How would you rate our reception desk?

1➡➡2➡➡➡3➡➡➡4➡➡➡5➡➡➡6➡➡➡7➡➡➡8➡➡➡9➡➡➡10

Unsatisfactory   Excellent

This is a condensed version of the type of questions asked. The actual resident satisfaction survey was thirty pages long with one question on each page and a place for comments.

Observations

An observation is made at the job site while employees are working. Its purpose is to determine how well they are able to perform a particular task or skill. You cannot observe feelings or attitudes, only behavior. It is therefore necessary for you to determine what kind of behavior you are looking for before you conduct this type of evaluation. A checklist will show you and the trainees what you observed and what needs to be worked on.

Observations can be formal or informal. A manager like Harry would do an informal observation by wandering by the employee's work station, exchanging a few encouraging comments and checking "ok" or "not ok" as to how well that employee performs. This is perhaps all he would need to evaluate the success or failure of the training effort. A manager like Samantha, on the other hand, would have a comprehensive, detailed observation guide and look for very specific behaviors. In fact, she would repeat the observation several times before deciding whether or not her employee was performing satisfactorily. There is a wide variety in the quality, detail, and type of information that can be collected from an observation. You need to decide how much detail is needed based on your situation. The observation is one of the most common methods for assessing performance.

Advantages of Observations

- In many cases, this is the *only* way to tell if employees are doing their jobs properly. By actually watching them on the job site, you can tell what they are able and willing to do. You need an observation guide to help you observe objectively and look for behaviors the employee was trained to do. Sometimes an employee is well trained and able to perform the task in the classroom, but does not do it on the job. There can be many causes for this lack of performance, such as insufficient motivation or environmental barriers. By evaluating the employee's training progress, other barriers may surface. We will talk about environmental barriers in more detail later.

- Trainees can learn at their own pace. Progress is recorded via the observation guide, which can help you work with the trainee to set goals.
- An observation can be used as pretest/posttest data to determine change in behavior, skill, or quality of a service. If managers can actually observe an improvement, they will be convinced by that more than by any other information. The guide helps identify the change.
- There are many ways to record observations:

    Videos are used occasionally for evaluation or training. Videos are used in training sessions as well as on the job to record progress. Some companies use videos continuously to scan operations.

    Journals are kept by some managers to record observations of employee performance on a regular basis. This could be used effectively following a training program to report changes or problems.

    Checklists are used as guides by many managers just to remind them what to look for and to make sure they notice the same things with each employee.

- Use your imagination. As a trainer you can create other methods to help you and others observe employee training and progress made.

Disadvantages to Observation

- Observations take time, and time is money. It takes a lot of your time, or someone's time, to observe employees on the job and record information regarding their performance.

- Observations can be subjective. Observers' views of what they see can be obscured by feelings about the employee being observed. Some employees can do no wrong, others may perform equally well but may not be rated the same. This has to do with a self-fulfilling prophesy. Managers have expectations of their employees, both positive and negative. Somehow they live up to these expectations. Or do they? Perhaps our preconceived notions cloud the real performance. A detailed checklist can help objectivity.
- The best way to make sure an observation is totally objective is to hire an outside observer, someone who will view all of your employees equally and judge them solely on performance.
- Some employees panic when they know they're being observed. They may become anxious and act differently than they would under ordinary circumstances. The reverse is also true. Some employees are on their best behavior when they know they are being observed. The observation may be the strongest factor that you rely on to evaluate performance, but it may not give you accurate information. The best way to deal with that is to plan many observations under various conditions. Let employees become accustomed to someone observing them so their true nature will emerge. Anyone can have a bad day—or a good one.

Sources for Observation

There are many people who can observe your employees and record information on their performance. If you feel your presence will change the situation, an outside observer might be more appropriate. Peers are in a position to observe employee behavior regularly. You must be tactful about how you ask for information so they don't feel their friends will get in trouble as a result of their reports. If peers regularly observe each other's skills with the intent of encouraging development, then you must reward teamwork.

Observation Example

A chain of West Coast food markets invested in customer service training for all of its cashiers. It identified specific behaviors that it wanted cashiers to use, such as greeting the customer, making eye contact, smiling, asking for coupons, etc.

It decided to evaluate the results of the training program by using secret shoppers. These were outside observers hired to act as customers. They shopped in the stores and went through the checkout lines in the usual manner. They were trained to look for the specific behaviors the cashiers were trained to do. They would then leave the store and rate the checker based on their observations. This method gave the training department objective data as to whether the employees were applying the techniques they learned in the classroom to the job.

The following page is an example of a secret shopper observation form.

Secret Shopper Observations for Cashiers

Did the cashier greet you when you approached the register?

   Yes ___ No ____

Comments _____
_____

Did the cashier make eye contact with you at any time during the transaction?

   Yes ___ No ____

Comments _____
_____

Did the cashier smile and portray a positive attitude?

   Yes ___ No ____

Comments _____
_____

Did the cashier call you by name?

   Yes ___ No ____

Comments _____
_____

Did the cashier invite you to use coupons?

   Yes ___ No ____

Comments _____
_____

Did the cashier respond to questions and requests?

   Yes ___ No ____

Comments _____
_____

Documents

Every company keeps some form of written records or documents. Some companies do a much better job than others, but even poorly kept records can give you information about training needs and how to evaluate them. Many training programs are started as a response to some form of documentation. Let's look at a few typical documents that lead to training efforts.

Performance appraisals may indicate areas where employees need improvement. If an employee is going to be downgraded on a performance appraisal, the company also needs to provide some way for that employee to improve. Frequently training is suggested. Maybe an outside consultant could be hired to design a program for several employees who are weak in the same area. If a single employee is identified as needing help in a specific area, then a coaching session or college class that is reimbursed by the company might be recommended.

Profit and loss documentation often leads to training. Companies are always trying to find ways to produce goods or services at higher quality and lower cost. This often means technical or skills training to improve speed or reduce errors and waste. Evaluating training is directly related to improvement in the bottom line, resulting in higher profits, lower costs or both.

Employee grievances, especially in a union environment, can cost the company time and money. Supervisory and management training often is provided as a response to complaints about how supervisors and managers are treating workers. If the grievances decrease after training, then those documents can be used to evaluate the results of training.

Customer complaints or response cards guide much of the training done in hotels and other service-based organizations. Your response as a customer tells them how they are doing and if training is needed. Recently, customers have become the primary source of information and feedback that guides an organization's direction.

Accident reports and OSHA inspections lead to required employee safety training. Evaluation of these programs varies according to the significance of the accidents. If it is a hazardous job with the possibility of serious accidents then safety training is extensive and evaluation of results is critical.

Based on typical documentation kept by every organization, there are many ways to assess a need for training and to evaluate its results.

Advantages of Using Documents

- They are already available. Every company keeps at least the five types of documents mentioned above. There are generally many more that are readily available to you as a source of information and a method of evaluation. In addition, someone else is gathering the data for you. I recommend checking the documents that are already kept by your organization before you "reinvent the wheel."
- Documents provide quantifiable data. If your client is a manager like Samantha and wants numbers and facts, organization documents provide that kind of numerical, objective data.
- The mere act of keeping records increases employee awareness of specific problems and can improve results. Many of you are familiar with the famous Hawthorne Studies. At the Western Electric plant in Hawthorne, Ohio, it was discovered that any change in the work environment created increased productivity—even lowering the lights and increasing the noise level. This baffled behavioral scientists until they realized that the attention paid to the employees by documenting their progress, regardless of other influencing factors, resulted in improved results. Any change caused temporary improvement and that improvement was a result of

employee attitude. This agrees with the principle that "what gets checked, gets done." Management gets what it checks, not what it expects.

- Documents are credible. Most people consider past records viable, reliable, verifiable information. Even when records are not complete or well-done, if they are dated and signed, they are credible.

Disadvantages of Using Documents

- Some records may be incomplete or inaccurate. You may not know by looking at a past record that it might have been carelessly or intentionally filled out incorrectly. Perhaps a manager had a personality conflict with an employee and downgraded that employee on a skill to express disapproval. That employee might be sent to training when, in fact, his or her skill was quite adequate. A court of law will accept employee records such as performance appraisals as verifiable data in a litigation. If managers fill them out in a casual manner, saying employees are okay when they are not, the employees may use those records as evidence against the company if disciplinary action is taken. In this case, the document could be a disadvantage. If a record system is in place, you may wish to update or improve it.

- If a record system is not in place for a specific area that you want to track, it may be difficult to establish one. It takes time and effort and people don't seem to have the time, even if they agree that a record system would be beneficial. Take this evaluation system, for example. Most managers agree that evaluation and follow-up to training would indeed make the training more effective and that transfer of learning would increase. However, they often balk at the idea that it is their responsibility—that they are the best ones to evaluate change as a result of training especially if this function was done by the training department in the past. They see it as one more chore added to their already busy schedules. This attitude prevails even when they agree that there is a clear benefit to the employees, to them and to the organization. Starting and keeping a new record system is generally resisted.

- No personal contact is made. Generally, when documents are used they are dug out of a file or anonymous responses are used. No effort is made to contact the people who filled out the report to determine what they meant by certain responses or how they interpreted the questions. This reminds me of a focus group I was part of to evaluate speakers for a convention. We had a showcase of several speakers and each of us evaluated them for the convention. There were several that I thought were very good and a few who were outstanding. One person in the focus group gave them all scores far below the rest of us. When questioned about his documentation, he replied, "I never give an outstanding or excellent. I think there is always room for improvement." Obviously, his interpretation of the question skewed the results of this small focus group. Unfortunately, an explanation by the person who filled out the document is generally not possible.

Data Sources for Documentation

You can go to anyone who keeps records. It might be someone in personnel, a secretary, department manager or a particular employee who likes to do such things. As long as the information is useful to you, tap into all possible resources. If it's dated and signed, it counts. It would be nice if it were also complete and accurate.

Documentation Example

A Japanese computer company settled in Los Angeles to manufacture computers. They hired American employees and proceeded to teach them the Japanese philosophy of Total Quality Management. They invited employee suggestions but were not getting many. They decided to start training with Quality Circles to increase employee suggestions.

Since the purpose of the Quality Circles was to increase employee suggestions, that is what the company measured.

The managers in each department simply kept track of the number of suggestions that came in each month to determine the value of the Quality Circles. They evaluated the quality of suggestions and ways to implement and reward good ones as well. However, they wanted to determine if the number of suggestions increased enough to make the Quality Circles worthwhile. For six months each department recorded its number of suggestions. Each employee suggestion was treated as a separate document which was kept in an appropriate file.

The evaluation form on the following page kept track of the number of employee suggestions that came from each department over the first six-month period.

Quality Circles—Employee Suggestions

	March	April	May	June	July	August
Accounting						
Personnel						
Purchasing						
Sales						
Shipping						
Customer Service						

Simulations

Simulations are exercises that trainees participate in to demonstrate the real thing. The simulations are planned to mimic problems or tasks that are faced on the job. Simulations probably present the greatest diversity and variety for evaluating training. Many organizations are producing board games, like Monopoly, to teach people specific operations. Here are a few examples of how games and simulations are used to teach, evaluate and simulate the skills that need to be acquired in training.

NASA uses a simulator to teach astronauts how to fly. The simulator is a big toy. It is a copy of a real spacecraft to give trainees an opportunity to learn, practice and be evaluated before allowing them to use the real thing. In this case, simulation of the actual experience is a crucial part of training and evaluation. How would you like to be in a plane where the pilot learned to fly through lecture and manuals without experiencing simulated exercise?

McDonald's uses a board game at McDonald University to teach trainees how a store operates. There are stations and steps—cards that are drawn with problems to solve. It is an interactive and entertaining alternative for training. It is fun and it works. I wonder how many realtors began their careers with a fascination for Monopoly as children?

GTE uses simulations in the form of role plays for supervisors to see if new telephone operators are ready to go on-line. When a new operator returns from customer service training, the supervisor pulls a CSC (Customer Service Card) from the file at random. The supervisor plays the role of the customer to see if the trainee is ready to handle the public or needs more training.

Advantages of Simulations and Games

- They have a wide variety of uses. A simulation can be used before a training program as a needs assessment to tell if a person really needs training. Simulations and games can be used during training programs. All of the simulations and games mentioned above are examples of training techniques that are (or could be) used during a training session to practice the intended skills. Simulations can also be used after training to evaluate results.

- Simulations can be created to evaluate the specific skill or concept that you are teaching. Again, there is no one right way. There is only a method that will give you the information you are looking for. You need to make sure that you base your simulation for evaluation on the skills that are actually taught in the training program. If supervisors or others evaluate your training, give them an evaluation instrument so they will evaluate only skills that were taught.

- Simulations and games can be used for all kinds of training. They are limited only by your creativity. Once you find a simulation that works, you can use it over and over. See if you can come up with a simulation or game that will test trainees' skills or knowledge.

- They are flexible. A simulation can take a few minutes or as much time as you feel is necessary to get your employees ready to handle the job. You can set up a simulation for several employees to participate in at once. You could create a simulation and have an experienced employee facilitate it for you. You could have employees suggest simulations or games that would demonstrate trainees' progress. Simulations and games can be bought "off the shelf."

- Simulations are fun and non-threatening. It is game playing. Most employees enjoy them. They add a light touch to "evaluation," which could diminish anxiety. If you were sent to a management development course, how would you choose to be evaluated on the results? Simulation is preferred by many of those who are being evaluated.

Disadvantages of Simulations

- The major disadvantage is whether or not the skills learned and demonstrated in a simulation will actually transfer under real conditions. Will those who are trained on earthquake preparedness be quite as cool and calm when faced with a real crisis? Those involved in a simulation know in the back of their minds that this is only "let's pretend." It is not the real thing. Ken, a friend and training manager, told me about the POW training he received as a Navy pilot in Viet Nam. He described the brutal treatment the trainees received. When asked how he got through it all, he said he saw some of his buddies "freak out" but he kept reminding himself it was only a game and in the end he would not really die, he would be okay.
- Creating a relevant, realistic simulation requires creativity, time and energy —not only to create the simulation, but to administer it. Trainees must be willing to participate to make it worthwhile and to give you the first-hand information you need. Consultants can create simulations for you, or you can purchase "off the shelf" games that are used in training programs.

Data Sources for Simulations

All those who play and watch—the employee, the supervisor, peers who might also be involved in the simulation and the trainer who taught the skill in the first place. An outside observer also can be used if objectivity is an important issue.

A Simulation Example

A Red Cross instructor was teaching a group of paramedic trainees how to administer first aid to drowning victims. There were ten paramedics taking turns with a dummy and then practicing with each other. They were learning how to push water out of the victim's lungs, give mouth-to-mouth resuscitation and administer electric shocks. They all did very well with the dummy, but had more difficulty with each other. Even though they knew that the reality of someone drowning was serious business, they couldn't help but laugh and fool around when trying to practice mouth-to-mouth with each other. The instructor warned that this was a technique they needed to learn and might mean life or death to someone at some time.

At the end of the training, they were evaluated on many skills. The evaluation for reviving a drowning victim was done with a simulation on a stranger. Afterwards, verbal feedback and written comments were made by the trainer and peers. Each time the simulation was slightly different to duplicate reality (i.e., different victims, different locations, different environmental distractions). In that way, each trainee had a unique situation to deal with. The evaluation form on the following page was used to collect information.

Drowning Simulation

- Scene is enacted where a paramedic is called to find a victim who had drowned. There's no time to collect information, only to administer emergency first aid. How does the trainee handle the situation?

Comment on...

Self-Control: _____

_____

_____

Followed Procedures: _____

_____

_____

Use of Equipment: _____

_____

_____

Response to Distractions: _____

_____

_____

Other Observations or Comments: _____

_____

_____

_____

_____

Action Plans

Action plans, sometimes called learning contracts, are developed by the participant at the end of a training program. They are one of my favorite forms of evaluation because they follow the adult learning theory that says adults learn what they are ready to learn. It lets the participants decide exactly what changes they will make based on the things they learned in training. When adults are in a learning situation, there is a wide variety of maturity, experience and interests brought into the session. People can learn valuable but different things, or they can learn the same thing but apply it differently. Action plans are designed to allow for participant flexibility.

Advantages of Action Plans

- Participants commit to changes that they are ready and willing to make. In any training session, adults are at different levels. There are those who have had little training; they are overwhelmed and mind-boggled by all the new ideas presented in a one-day seminar. An action plan helps them sort the information, prioritize, choose a few bite-size chunks to work on, and not be overwhelmed on where to begin. There are those who are seasoned professionals but still willing to learn some new techniques. During training, they are looking for and generally find some "ahas." However, these ideas seem to fly away if they are not recorded. The action plan serves as a "keeper sheet" and reminder for the good ideas they want to remember. There are some employees who don't want to go to training, don't want to make changes, don't want to disrupt the status quo. For those people, an action plan serves as a motivator. If they're required to choose a few things they're willing to try, they're less resistant. Especially if they know their bosses will be checking up on them. The greatest advantage of the action plan is giving participants flexibility to make commitments they are ready for.

- Action plans are easy to develop. They can be generic because they take form through the person filling in the blanks. They also give you great flexibility in how you will follow-up. You or the trainee's manager can casually review the action plan by wandering around. You can ask selected people to come to your office and discuss their plans with you. Managers can collect copies of each action plan to help with performance appraisals. A less desirable, but possible, technique is to assign someone else to check the action plans — a "buddy system."

- Action plans can be formal or informal. I recommend the informal kind shown in the sample. Sometimes they are given more structure by the trainer filling in the areas they want addressed; the participants add the rest. A learning contract is a much more formal type of action plan. It is an agreement or commitment made between the trainees and the instructor or their supervisors as to the changes that will be made. The progress that is expected is outlined step-by-step with dates for each progression. Someone is in charge of following up with each step at the agreed-upon date. This agreement is actually signed by the trainees and the person who follows their progress. This is a formal agreement and is frequently used with self-study programs where new trainees are expected to learn certain procedures on their own.

Disadvantages of the Action Plan

- The major disadvantage of the action plan is a big one: More than any other evaluation technique, it requires a commitment to follow-up. There are a few, very few, self-motivated people who will go to a training session, learn new things, mentally commit to change, and then do it on their own. Most people need to know that someone out there notices and cares. Think of the times you have gone to conventions. You probably attended at least a half-dozen breakout sessions or workshops where you got some great ideas. Perhaps the workshop provided an action plan. Now think how many of those ideas actually got implemented. It might have been different if your boss asked to see your action plan and followed-up on it. If you expect changes to occur from action plans, you arrange for follow-up on them. If you cannot, use a different form of evaluation.

- Another disadvantage can be the environment. Occasionally, those well-meaning employees who really would make changes on their own are sabotaged by their environment. Again, they need you or their supervisor to step in and help so they can achieve their goals. Peers may be the problem here, especially if one was trained and the rest were not. Peer pressure to resist change and maintain the status quo may be great. Training works best from the top down and when all who are involved are included in the training effort.

Data Sources for Action Plans and Learning Contracts

The employee who was trained is the only one who can fill out an action plan or learning contract. However, to make it work, someone else must support it. The best person is the employee's supervisor. Occasionally, contracts are made with trainers or with peers who agree to follow-up and motivate each other.

Action Plan Example

A county court system wanted a management/supervisory program for Levels III and IV clerks. Several small courts got together and hired a consultant to design a basic soup-to-nuts program for their supervisors. It included ten half-day modules delivered every other week for ninety participants. Five different instructors facilitated the modules. Each module was linked to the next with an action plan. Here's how it worked: At the end of a module, the facilitator would have the participants fill in three things they would be willing to work on in the next two weeks. The next instructor began by reviewing action-plan items. This provided continuity from week to week and let trainers know how participants were doing.

Their supervisors and the court administrators were given a session on how to evaluate the training based on action plans. They were told to periodically walk around and ask to see an action plan, to talk to the trainees about what they were working on, and offer assistance if necessary. The objective was to show management interest, lend support to the program, and encourage those who were making progress. The administrators liked this method because it was flexible for them and required no paperwork, but still gave the information they needed on how the training was going. One court administrator actually had his assistant follow-up each session with a meeting with each participant to encourage the transfer process. The action plan on the following page is an example of this informal method used with the county courts.

Action Plan

- List three things from today's training session that you will work on in the next two weeks. Be prepared to discuss them with your administrator.

1) Action: _____
   _____
   _____
   _____

2) Action: _____
   _____
   _____
   _____

3) Action: _____
   _____
   _____
   _____

Tracking Charts

Tracking charts are simply a way of keeping score, which people love to do because it gives them a way to compete. They can be used on an individual basis to keep score on yourself—like in golf, where you compete with your own best effort. They can also be used for teams to keep score on each other. Keeping score is highly motivational. We all have our own methods of keeping score that let us or the world know how well we are doing.

Tracking charts were used extensively in the 40s when time/motion studies were being done in factories to improve productivity. Charts were kept as small changes were made on production lines and in the environment. This same idea has gained new life as TQM (Total Quality Management) has become a current buzzword. Whether it is Juran, Crosby or Demming, it is everywhere—and it keeps score. Many factories use SPC (Statistical Process Control) to help keep score. The tracking charts used with Total Quality Management are directly related to employee training in various areas.

While tracking charts look very different, they have two things in common: players are identified and progress over time is recorded. This means there must be a time limit. You can't track indefinitely, but you can end and start over. There must be culmination, an ending when you count and celebrate—or plan a new attack.

Advantages of Tracking Charts

- Tracking charts are great motivators that make work into a game. We all learned to enjoy games as children, and in games we kept score. Why not build on that positive attitude of fun and game playing in the work environment?
- Tracking charts provide constant feedback. When someone keeps score—an employee, a work team, a department—a company knows exactly where it stands

compared to its own record, trends in the industry, or with its competition. One of the complaints heard most frequently from employees is that they don't get enough feedback from their supervisors. Even if that feedback is not good, it is better than not knowing. Managers often resist giving feedback to employees because it is time consuming and they're not good at verbalizing it. Tracking charts are an easy way to give ongoing feedback.

Management trainer and consultant Bill Daniels describes how to use tracking charts to motivate employees. You ask each employee to determine what is a fair day's work for a fair day's pay. You keep track of the work done each day, then feed back the information to the employees and reward achievement. He says the feedback itself is rewarding.

- Tracking charts provide variety. There are many ways to keep score. Some people use bar graphs, others prefer pie charts, while line graphs may be the choice of others. You can create your own score card or tracking chart. Use whatever works best.

- Tracking charts can be private. If you simply want to improve the performance or productivity of a specific individual, try keeping a tracking chart with that person. A perfect example would be with our easygoing manager, Harry, who wanted to help David get out of his sales slump. Harry could keep a tracking chart with David after sending him to training. Because David's confidence was low and he is generally a star performer, this chart would be confidential between Harry and David.

- Tracking charts clarify goals and priorities. When a chart is kept, there is no doubt in anyone's mind about what is top priority. After sending a few selected employees to a management training program, one manager started keeping track of newly generated ideas. His priorities for his group were made very clear. He wanted to know if those who attended this training program came up with more new ideas than they did before or if they developed more new ideas than those who were not sent to training. He actually posted a small graph on the inside of his office window so those concerned would have to be interested enough to find it. However, just by virtue of his keeping track, his priorities and goals were well known to those who worked for him.

Disadvantages of Tracking Charts

- They have a limited shelf life. After a while, the novelty wears off and they are no longer motivational. The longest a tracking chart should go is three years. Most are for short term programs like our examples. When using them, think about how long your enthusiasm and that of your employees can be maintained for this particular project.
- There must be a meaningful reward at the end of the road for those involved. To play, they must want to win. A city went to great effort to work with its union and figure out an incentive program for employees based on performance appraisals. The negotiations and redesign of the performance appraisal program and forms took months. Finally, they agreed on a three-step merit plan based on performance. As we were training the city department managers and supervisors on how the new program would operate, something became apparent. They now had a pay incentive to encourage managers to do better performance appraisals and motivate their workers to do better work. However, when the numbers were actually tallied, those at the highest of the three steps would receive $300 per year more than those at the lowest. Some of the supervisors decided it wasn't worth it to "bust their butts" all year for $300. This ended up as a negative reinforcement for them and encouraged them to maintain the status quo.
- S*omeone* must be in charge of keeping score. The data for the tracking chart must be collected, tallied and posted regularly throughout the program. Someone must agree

to do it. It does not need to be you, but if you assign someone, you must realize some of his time will be spent doing it.

- One more disadvantage. I've had arguments with colleagues on the value of internal versus external motivation. Tracking charts do not encourage the philosophy that people should work for the love of work, rather than for a specific prize. If you adhere to that philosophy, then tracking charts will not appeal to you. Some people are motivated by tracking their own progress and rewarding themselves for accomplishing goals. Tracking charts mostly bank on the external reward as a motivator. Again, you have options; tracking charts are just one.

Data Sources for Tracking Charts

Employees can keep their own tracking charts. You, or their supervisor, can keep one on areas you wish to make known as priorities. An employee can be assigned to keep score, or an external person in Personnel, HRD or Accounting who has access to the numbers can keep the chart.

Example of Tracking Charts

A distribution center for a large winery was providing training for district managers. Each district manager was responsible for a certain area in the city. The territories were divided based on past records so that sales from each area were about equal. The district managers sent their sales representatives for in-house sales training. Since the trainer was hired because he was one of the best, they were confident their sales reps were well trained in class. The brunt of the training was left to the district managers, on the job. The company decided to motivate district managers and their sales teams with a contest. The prize was a trip on a cruise ship. A huge tracking chart, like the one in the example, was placed in the employee lunch room. It was based on sales in their areas and lasted three months. All members of the team that had the best record were given a four-day cruise for two with their district manager.

Needless to say, the district managers started some heavy duty on-the-job training to inspire their teams. The investment the company made was easily covered in profits from increased sales, goodwill and enthusiasm from the sales reps, and renewed energy in the on-the-job training the district managers provided.

Each week the controller, who kept track of the number of cases of wine sold, recorded the results on the tracking chart.

Tracking Chart

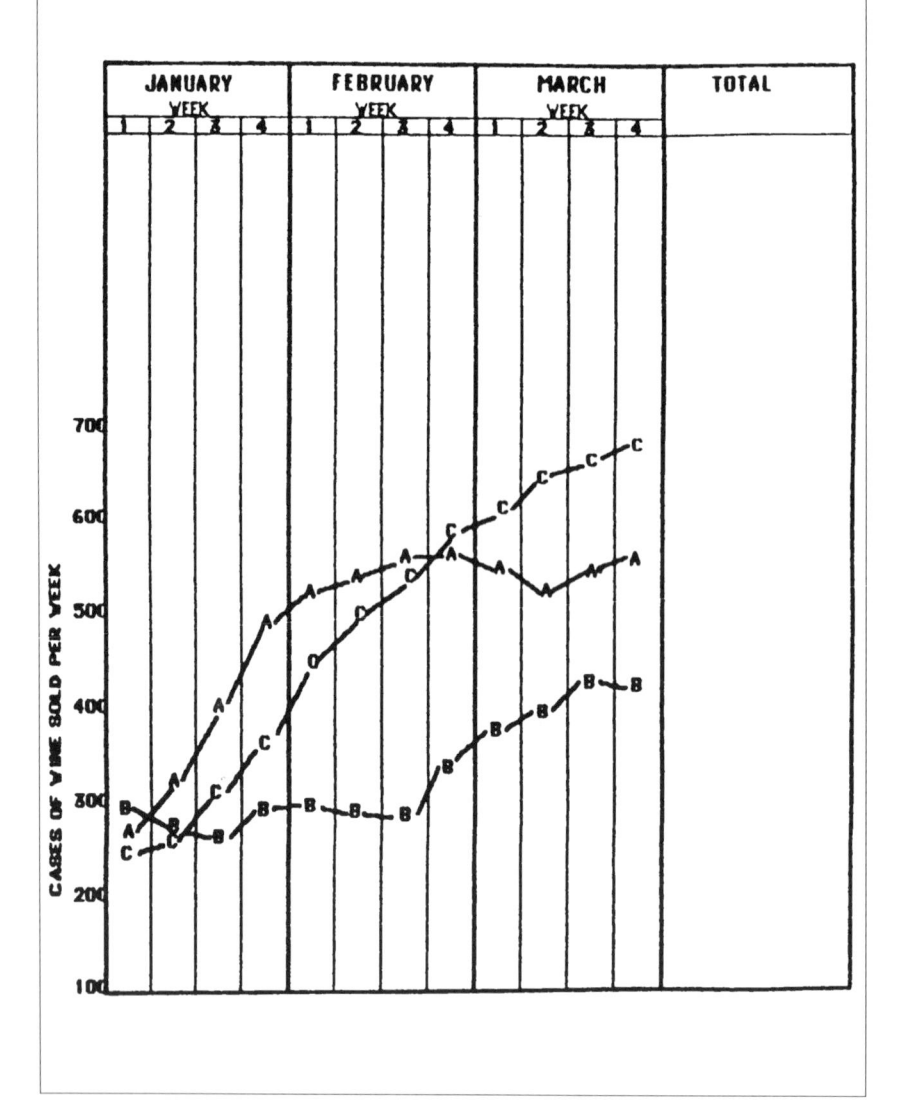

	JANUARY WEEK				FEBRUARY WEEK				MARCH WEEK				TOTAL
	1	2	3	4	1	2	3	4	1	2	3	4	

CASES OF WINE SOLD PER WEEK

Tracking Chart

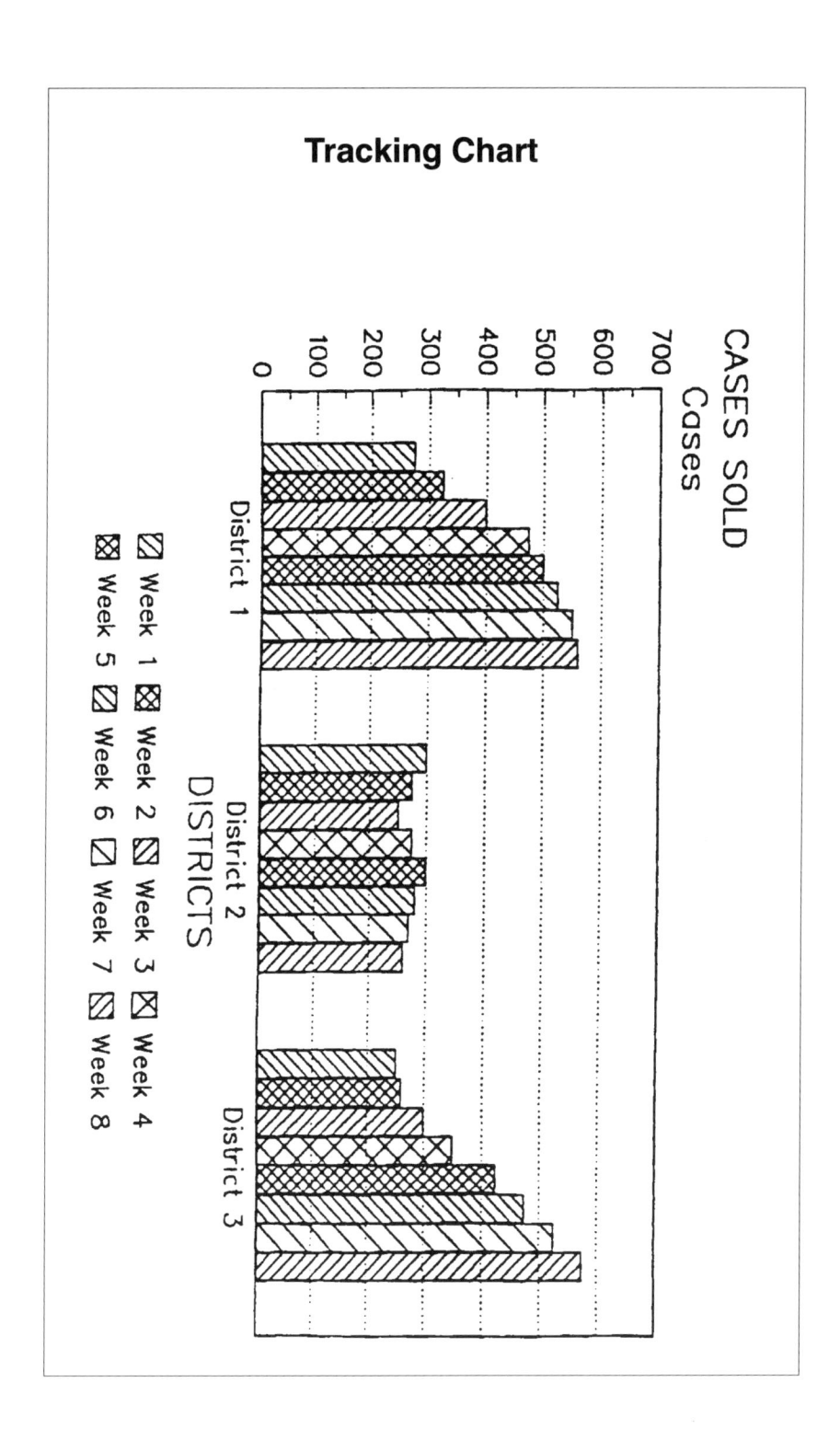

Gap Analysis Checklist

A gap analysis checklist is developed by determining "what is" and "what needs to be." It is based on individual competencies and helping trainees become competent in identified skills. Its purpose is to help trainees improve by finding out what they can do, checking them off if they are okay, then training on what still needs to be improved. It is especially useful when someone needs to be certified or competent in several areas before being allowed to face the public or practice in the field. It is a developmental process where 100 percent efficiency is the goal, but not immediately after training. The checklist allows trainees to develop at their own pace, realizing that some trainees enter a program with more skills than others. Once they are checked off as competent in all the areas on the list, attention no longer needs to be focused on that employee. Your time needs to be devoted to those who need reinforcement in order to bring them up to standards. The checklist allows you to focus on small steps in the evaluation and development of employees. Some checklists are sequenced and follow a precise progression, others simply check off "can they or can't they?" do something. The checklist records progress—the goal is to have employees competent in all items on the list and checked off.

The checklist appeals to managers like Pete, who view training as a developmental process with small steps leading to competence.

Ideally, rewards are given when a trainee has successfully demonstrated competence and completed all of the items on the checklist.

Advantages of the Gap Analysis Checklist

- The list can be private, with an individual developmental plan for each trainee and his or her supervisor. It can be public, a guide for a team of trainees to work on together to motivate and assist each other. When it is used in that way, it becomes a competitive game, which is okay if it is monitored and for the expressed purpose of building a team with everyone becoming 100 percent competent. There is no reward for being first, but a big reward for becoming competent.

- Trainees can learn in small sequential steps and are evaluated as they complete each step. It allows for the vast difference in skills and aptitudes that are encountered when dealing with adults. They can learn at their own pace when the only value judgment being made is whether or not they are competent or need additional training.
- The gap analysis checklist can be as detailed as desired. It is criterion reference rather than norm reference. Each criterion on it could have several steps to accomplish and deadlines for rechecking each item. Or it could be self-directed, where the trainees indicate their readiness to be checked.
- The checklist helps trainees set goals and gives them priorities to work on. The items on the checklist must be based on what was actually learned in training. Rewards that are predetermined provide incentives for accomplishing goals.
- The results are measurable. If trainees are checked off, you can assume they are able to demonstrate that skill. Whether or not they use it in the field is a different problem.

Disadvantages of Gap Analysis Checklists

- Evaluation is limited to the items on the checklist. The supervisor or whoever is in charge of monitoring the trainee rarely looks for or evaluates skills, abilities, competencies, knowledge, etc. if they are not listed.

They tend to focus on the items mentioned and do not notice others that may in fact be relevant to success in the field but were not addressed on the checklist.

- Checklists provide guidelines. To work well, the records must be kept accurately and follow-up dates attended to. If trainees are not checked off on a particular item, there needs to be a specific date set when they will be rechecked and developmental opportunities provided so that progress can be made. In the meantime, the trainees should be practicing the skills that were okayed. They will be forgotten if not used.

- This method can become very rigid or inconsistent depending on the evaluator. There must be an effort made to ensure that all of the evaluators are consistent. This is the same problem that exists with performance appraisals. If employees are demonstrating skills for one supervisor and are checked off, it is assumed that they would be checked off no matter who was doing the evaluation.

Data Sources for Gap Analysis Checklists

The employees can be evaluated by anyone who can understand the items on the checklist. It could be you, or their supervisor, a peer or an outside observer. This is an evaluation method with many opportunities for delegation.

Example of Gap Analysis Checklist

A major auto manufacturer puts a great deal of time, money and effort into training district managers to ensure a positive relationship between dealerships and corporate headquarters. The district managers are brought in from all over the country for a two-week basic training program. During the two weeks, they cover consultive selling, customer service, interpreting financial statements and other skills that will prepare them to assist dealers. The new district managers are overwhelmed by all the new information given to them during their training. The trainers are well aware that the real training takes place when they return to the job and have an opportunity to try their new skills.

When district managers return from training, the regional managers start with on-the-job training. As the district manager progresses, the regional manager checks off areas the district manager has accomplished and areas that need help. Sometimes the regional manager, personally, is in a position to train the district manager. Generally, the gaps are filled by other experienced district managers. Occasionally, a manual or self-study program is recommended. The objective is to make sure the investment in bringing the district managers together for basic training pays off with competent district managers in the field.

A training session for their regional managers is provided to prepare them to follow-up, evaluate and continue on-the-job development. The checklist in the example is one page from a twelve-page manual that helps regional managers guide their district managers' progress.

Gap Analysis Checklist

1. Ability to assist dealers to achieve good CSI performance in the dealerships

Yes	Needs Improvement	Can Your DMs Do the Following:
		* Analyze and prioritize customer satisfaction information?
		* Encourage dealers to post results?
		* Encourage dealers to convey corporate guidelines on customer service for dealership employees?
		* Help dealers design a compensation plan for employees tied to customer satisfaction results?
		* Discuss customer satisfaction information in regular department manager meetings?
		* Recommend customer relations training for appropriate dealership employees?
		* Close a consumer affairs report on the datanet system and teach dealers how to use the system?
		* Advise and counsel dealers with low customer satisfaction scores?
		* Develop an action plan to improve?
		* Follow-up the action plan to see that the commitment is carried out?

Gap Analysis Checklist

2. Analyze and evaluate dealership performance using financial statements and develop corrective action

Yes	Needs Improvement	Can Your DMs Do the Following:
		* Explain key elements to you prior to making a dealer contact?
		* Mention positive results as well as areas needing attention?
		* Recognize and understand each dealer's cash flow problems?
		* Make appropriate recommendations for improvement?
		* Discuss trends in composite group, district and region?
		* Is the District Manager sensitive to the need for confidentiality?
		* Use financial statements and expense guidelines as a basis for financial discussions?
		* Is the District Manager able to evaluate department productivity using Basic Training Worksheets?
		* Identify financial red flags and help devise action plans?
		* Follow-up on previous financial action plan items?

Chapter 5. The Link

All of those choices are a little mind boggling. How do you know which source and which method to use for which situation?

The *link* is designed to help you make that choice by considering your needs assessment and program objectives.

Asking yourself a few questions should help you choose an appropriate method for evaluation.

Making the Link

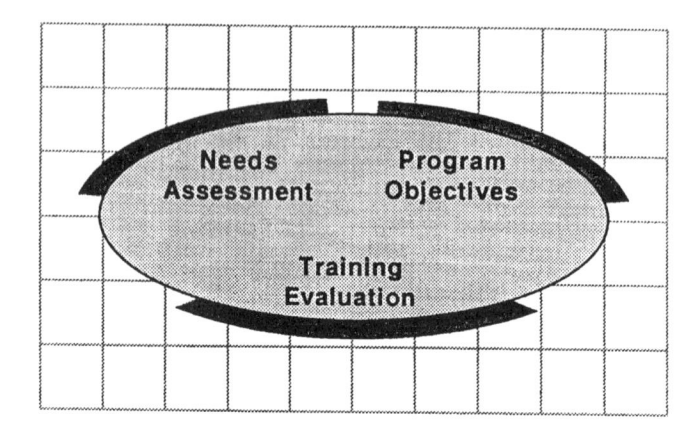

- **Needs Assessment = WHY**
  Why do we need this program?
  Why do employees need this skill?

- **Program Objectives = WHAT**
  What kind of results do we expect?
  What are the objectives of the training?

- **Training Evaluation = HOW**
  How do we know if it worked?
  How do we evaluate the results of
  the training?

Each of these parts that link together in evaluation will be discussed. The needs assessment determines your program objectives. The program objectives determine what to evaluate. The evaluation data links with future needs assessment, and so on...

Needs Assessment

This question is simply, "Why do we need this program?" Why are we spending time and money to train this person in this area? Needs generally fall into three categories.

Trainees have a need. Either they have been downgraded on a performance appraisal, they are not carrying their weight on the team, they requested help in a certain area, etc. The point is that they are "here" and need to be "there." Their skill, knowledge, or attitude is not up to par; these people need to improve.

> *Example*: Carla is a supervisor at the County Library. She was satisfied with her job and holding her own in spite of working late regularly to keep ahead of the job load. She said there just were not enough hours in the day for her small staff. The handful of young temporary employees did not get the job done because as soon as they were trained, they left. Besides, they fooled around a lot, and she had to check their work to make sure it was right. At performance appraisal time, Carla was given a low score on her ability to delegate and develop others. Her manager recommended a seminar on delegation and developing staff that the county provided. She and her manager agreed that her manager would follow-up to see if her skills had improved. The manager also agreed to re-evaluate her performance appraisal in three months and change the low rating if Carla's skills improved. Carla attended the seminar. She learned how to delegate and changed her behavior on the job. She learned how to train her young employees and understand their motivation for working. She also learned to back off and accept a mistake now and then. Although Carla must force herself to leave at closing time, she does. Her manager followed up the training, noted her progress and acknowledged it with a new performance appraisal.

The department has a need. Often training is provided based on a group need. A whole department might need team building. Sending one person would not do the trick even if that person was the weak link. The whole team must participate. Sometimes future needs are identified and departments or groups are trained to actively address a long-range plan. Sometimes it is in response to change.

> *Example*: An insurance company started with two partners and two phones. As the company grew, a receptionist, secretary and three new sales reps were hired. Their small phone system did not suffice. Their long-range plan was to continue to grow, and they decided to use a voice mail system. The phone company that sold them the system also sent someone to train all those who would use it. The training session included phone etiquette as well as technical information on using the system. The fact that this training session was included played a large part in the owners' decision to choose this voice mail system. The owners were provided follow-up forms to see if their people were using the telephone etiquette techniques and using the system to its full potential. This gave information to the phone company on how to improve its training program. It also was a guide to the owners. It let them know if their employees were using the new phone system properly.

"They" have a need. Some training is mandated from outside the department, even outside the organization. The federal government mandates hazardous waste training or safety training for certain business categories. The CEO attended a personal development workshop and mandates it for all managers. The executive committee wants the company to become more customer oriented and mandates training for all employees. Someone outside and higher up has dictated the need for training.

Example: The State of California decided all companies in a certain category must train their employees on earthquake preparedness. This was good news for outside vendors in the training field, who quickly put together programs, brochures and seminars on earthquake preparedness. At great expense, companies with thousands of employees embarked on this program. I was consulting with a phone company at the time and walked in one morning to find chaos. There were paramedics, fire trucks and what looked like dead and injured bodies all over the place. Others were walking around trying to care for them. This was a simulation, a very realistic simulation. If there is an earthquake in California, the safest place to be is at your local phone company! Are we able to evaluate the results of this training? I hope not! We can only evaluate the results of the simulation training.

What is the need for training? The reason for doing this, spending this time and money, will guide you toward how you will evaluate results. It simply answers the question *why*. *Why* do we need this? If you have a good answer, your program is probably worth conducting and the results worth evaluating. The *why* must also be cross-checked with department goals. Is this training consistent with the organization's strategic plan?

Program Objectives

The second part of the link asks the question *what?* What is being taught in this particular training program? It requires some accountability on the part of managers who send employees to training to know what their employees need and what they will learn there. It is not practical or necessary for them to attend every program they send employees to. They should, however, have some idea of what the program is about, what the main objectives are, if it matches their department needs and if it matches the employees' needs.

The training department must take responsibility to provide information about their programs to managers and a method to see if a particular program meets their needs.

Managers must have their department goals in mind first. See if this particular program will help meet them. If they do not make this *link*, employees could spend time learning new ideas that managers won't support. Find out what they need to meet their goals before providing training.

> *Example*: Sandy is a manager who sent her employees to a communication skills program because she wanted them to be better listeners. The in-house program, however, trained them on public speaking; listening was a very small part of it. The manager gave the program a poor evaluation. Even though the employees improved their presentations, she could see no significant improvement in their listening skills.

Part of the picture frame is based on what is actually being taught in the program. What did your trainees learn? It is not fair to them, or those providing the training, to evaluate them on what managers would like them to learn rather than on what they actually learned.

Here is another example of a gap between what was learned and what was evaluated. I was asked to design an evaluation tool for a problem-solving program. I reviewed the curriculum, which contained information on problem-solving methods A, B, C and D. As a consultant, I sat in on the program to learn what the students learned. I found the trainer zipped through methods A, B and C, and spent most of the time on method D. It would not be fair to evaluate the trainees on four methods of problem solving when they only learned one. It might help to find out from the trainees exactly what was taught. If the trainer is not delivering what was promised, this needs to be addressed.

Evaluation

With evaluation you start at the end, with the results you want from training. Then you work with your client, who will receive the evaluation data, to determine your best method. Based on the needs and the program objectives, you'll be able to choose which data source and method you will use. You will probably find several suitable combinations. Now consider management style. Is your client like Samantha, Pete or Harry? If you are dealing with a Samantha, you will probably want to use two or three evaluation methods and document each to get triangulation and verify results. Pete might want two methods for the trainees he needs to reinforce. If you are working with a Harry, one method will probably be fine.

The advantage of the On-Target system is that it offers you options. As long as you get the information you need, the system will work for you and your managers.

Give it a try with the worksheet on page 100. Think of one of your training programs. Ask yourself *why* the employee needs that particular program. Now, consider the program objectives. Do you have clear objectives for *what* your trainee will learn and the results you want? If you don't, *how* can you evaluate if they did or did not achieve the results? Now look at the On-Target Evaluation Chart on page 31 and mark the possible combinations of data sources and methods that could work for this program. See if you can find two or three you might actually want to use. Work with your client and trainees to choose the best one.

To summarize, the *link* will help you choose which data sources and methods to use in creating your evaluation instrument. It will help you create the proper frame for your picture.

- *By asking **why**?* Why are we providing this program? You can determine need. You can avoid providing programs on the latest fad for those who don't need them. You can also determine how elaborate your evaluation should be. A short training program should have an equivalent evaluation and follow-up. An elaborate program that costs a great amount of time, effort and money deserves a greater investment in evaluation and follow-up.

- *By asking **what**?* What is included in this training program? Managers can determine if this is the best program for their employees. They can get a clear picture of what is and what is not being taught, so that their expectations of results are realistic.

- *By asking **how**?* How should we follow-up and evaluate? You can combine data sources and methods to discover several possibilities. The answers to *why* and *what* will help you choose. So will understanding management style and what motivates employees. Together, you and your client, the managers who send their employee to your programs, can create a frame that perfectly fits the picture.

Training Program Link

Program: Delegation and Developing Staff

Employee: Carla

Needs Assessment: *Why* are we doing this?
How did you determine the need for this type of training?

    Reviewing performance appraisals

    Request from supervisor

    Request from employee

Program Objectives: *What* is being taught?
List three objectives of the training:

    1. How to train and develop employees

    2. Understanding motivation

    3. Techniques for delegation

Evaluation: *How* do we know it worked?
Use the Evaluation Chart to determine how you could measure results.

1. Method:	Personal documents on turnover and performance appraisals	
Source:	Supervisor	
2. Method:	Observation and checklist	
Source:	Trainee working with employees	
3. Method:	Interview	
Source:	Employees	

Training Program Link

Program:　Voice Mail

Employee:　All

Needs Assessment: *Why* are we doing this?
How did you determine the need for this type of training?

> New system needed
>
> Consistency in phone etiquette needed

Program Objectives: *What* is being taught?
List three objectives of the training:

> 1. How to use voice mail
>
> 2. Good phone etiquette
>
> 3. How to use other options

Evaluation: *How* do we know it worked?
Use the Evaluation Chart to determine how you could measure results.

> 1. Method:　Observation—for etiquette
>   Source:　All who use phone
>
> 2. Method:　Check list on programming voice mail
>   Source:　All who use phone
>
> 3. Method:　Survey
>   Source:　Those who use other options

Training Program Link

Program: Earthquake Preparedness

Employee: State Employees

Needs Assessment: *Why* are we doing this?
How did you determine the need for this type of training?

    Mandated by the state

Program Objectives: *What* is being taught?
List three objectives of the training:

    1. What to do if a quake occurs

    2. How to administer basic first aid

    3. How to control panic

Evaluation: *How* do we know it worked?
Use the Evaluation Chart to determine how you could measure results.

    1. Method: Questionnaire
       Source: Sample of employees

    2. Method: Interview
       Source: Discussion with all employees on staff

    3. Method: Simulation
       Source: Consultant or trainer

Training Program Link

Your Program: _____

Your Employee: _____

Needs Assessment: *Why* are we doing this?
How did you determine the need for this type of training?

_____

_____

_____

Program Objectives: *What* is being taught?
List three objectives of the training:

    1. _____

    2. _____

    3. _____

Evaluation: *How* do we know it worked?
Use the Evaluation Chart to determine how you could measure results.

    1. Method: _____
       Source: _____

    2. Method: _____
       Source: _____

    3. Method: _____
       Source: _____

Chapter 6. The Process

The *process* is how evaluation can be used as a tool to make learning transfer from the classroom to the work site. There are three crucial steps to make the process effective. This is where a bolt of the obvious strikes. It only took me four years and a Ph.D. dissertation to figure out how important this process is to the transfer of learning. This seems simple, but is important!

- ***Before*** sending employees to training, you need to *coach and counsel* to prepare them for training.
- ***During*** their transition period, when they are practicing new skills, you need to *address environmental barriers.*
- ***After*** training, to ensure that the gain is maintained, you need to *reward and reinforce progress.*

This is the point where trainers and managers can really make a difference. The process is flexible: You determine how much time you are willing and able to put into it, and which employees need more of your time and attention.

The Process Chart

The process chart puts the transfer of learning into perspective. It can be used with any training or development program. While evaluation instruments can change, the process remains the same. The most important issue in the transfer of learning is not the program itself. It is what occurs before and after that determines how much of the program transfers to the work site.

Managers often think of training in terms of "sending caterpillars in and expecting butterflies to come out." The training program is more like the cocoon; the butterfly will emerge on the job if the environment does not create too many barriers.

The process chart shows your program and evaluation instrument as input, with transfer of learning as the output. The process includes coaching and counseling that take place before training, addressing barriers when people return to the work site, and providing rewards and reinforcement when the program is finished.

Evaluation provides information and will help you with each of these areas. If you follow this simple three-step process, you will get more value from the time and money invested in training.

INPUTS

(Training Programs + Evaluation Instrument)

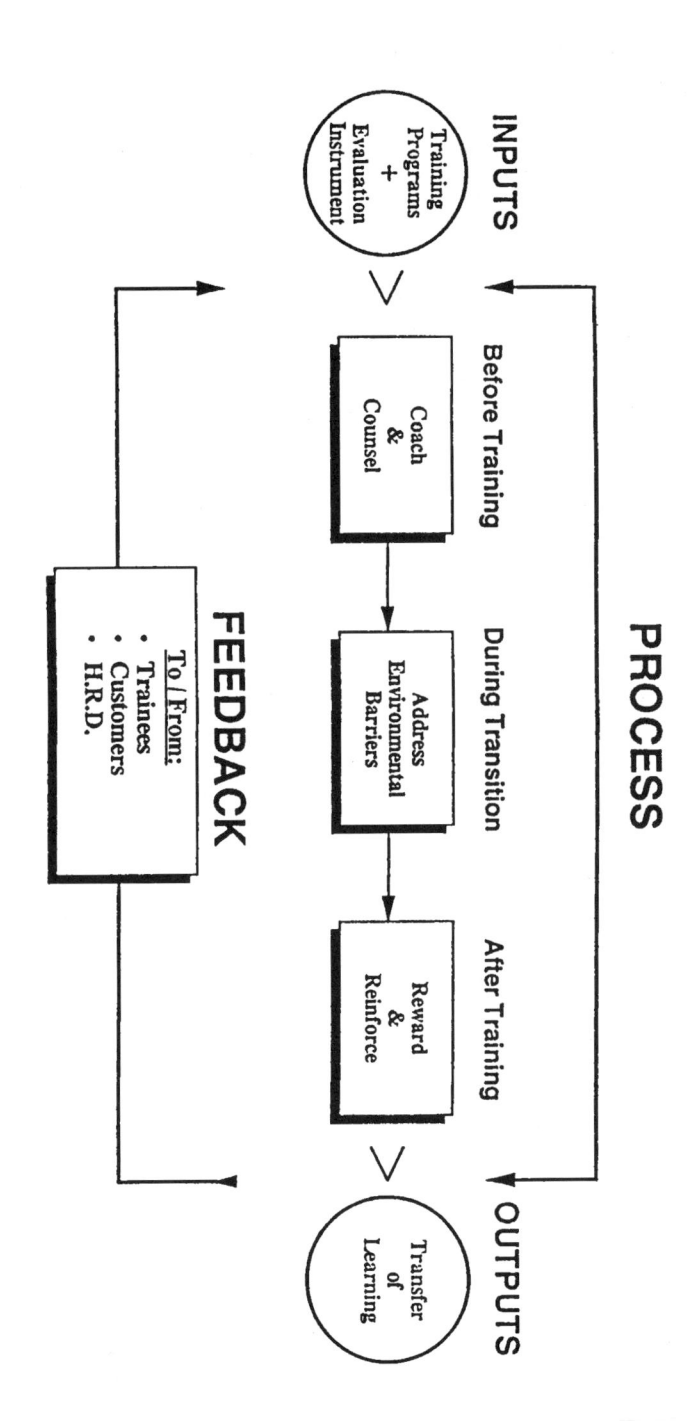

PROCESS

Before Training → Coach & Counsel

During Transition → Address Environmental Barriers

After Training → Reward & Reinforce

FEEDBACK

To / From:
- Trainees
- Customers
- H.R.D.

OUTPUTS

(Transfer of Learning)

Step I—Before Training: Coach and Counsel

Before sending an employe to training, there are important things that can be done to make training more effective. A coaching and counseling session opens trainees' minds, and prepares them for what they will learn. It is called an "advanced organizer." It provides an opportunity to think about what is coming and hook it on to what they already know. In a five-minute session, you or managers can coach trainees before sending them to training by discussing these issues:

1. *Why are they attending this training session?* What is the need? Let them know how this program, the skills they will learn, fits into the total picture or plans for the employees, the department and the organization. Training is not a stand-alone event: It is an organizational investment. It is part of where the organization is headed. This particular program may be a small part, but it fits into the total picture. If the employees have requested training, then this should also be understood. Have you noticed a lack of skill or a problem they are having? Is it time to prepare them for another step? Are you downsizing or do they need cross-training? Think about why the organization is investing the time and money to train these people, and make it clear to them.

Most of the time, employees don't know why they were sent to training. I have often stood in front of a group as an outside consultant and opened the session by asking, "Why are you here today?" Most of the time I get bewildered looks, shrugged shoulders, and comments like, "My boss sent me, I don't know why" or, "I received a memo in my box; my boss signed it." How can these trainees know what they are supposed to learn, or how they are supposed to change when they return to their jobs, if they don't even know why they were asked to attend? So, explain to employees why they were recommended for each program they attend. Why the organization was willing to invest time and money in their development.

2. ***What are the expectations?*** What do you expect them to learn in this program? More importantly, what do managers expect them to bring back to their department? What changes would you like to see as a result of training? If trainees know in advance what they are expected to learn, what they are expected to bring back, what their supervisors will notice, it would make a tremendous difference in how they approach the learning experience. Occasionally, trainers will try to fill that gap. They start a session by asking participants to list what they expect to get out of the program. Frequently, the participants don't know. It is difficult to relate learning in a classroom to a work situation, even when trainees know what to expect. It is almost impossible when they have not discussed training with the manager and don't know what they are expected to learn.

3. ***Do managers support the program?*** Let employees know their managers are aware of what will be covered—that they have read the class outline and believe this program will meet the employee's needs. This puts a responsibility in the hands of HRD to provide all managers with an accurate outline of every course they expect employees to attend. It puts accountability on manager's shoulders to read the course outline or find out from others what the class is all about. How can they motivate employees, create enthusiasm in them, if they don't have it themselves?

If the employees' supervisors do not support the training and do not plan to support the employees when they return to their department, don't waste their time. If the program is mandated and you don't support it, you need to have a long talk with yourself and then with your boss. If you must train employees on a program you don't support, such as one mandated by the government, be frank and up front in a coaching session with them. They will appreciate your candor and be prepared to put the whole thing in perspective.

4. ***How will you follow-up and evaluate results?*** The most important element in the transfer process is follow-up. How do you intend to reinforce this training? This is where the On-Target Evaluation Chart comes in. Use the chart as you or their manager discuss the pending program with the employee. Fill out the employee's name, the class they will attend, and the date. Then, in a coaching, counseling, collaborative discussion, discuss the method for follow-up. Together you will choose a date for follow-up. Since you collaborated with employees, they will not resist providing the data you agree to. In fact, if you get buy-in from them, they will remind you about the follow-up. After all, if they are making an effort to change, they certainly want you and their manager to know and give them credit for their efforts.

The evaluation method and follow-up date should be determined before the employee attends the training program. It works best when it is a collaborative agreement between you, the manager and the employee. It should give managers any information they want concerning the value of the program and how well the employee is doing as a result of attending.

You can fill in the box with an appropriate agreed-upon date. Some training can be measured immediately after it occurs. Other training takes longer before you can measure results. For example, if clerks are learning a new file system, they could demonstrate their knowledge immediately. If they are required to use it often, there are many opportunities to measure ability. If, on the other hand, a year-long management training program is required, you cannot expect immediate results. If the organization's intent is to cut down grievances filed against management, then it will take even longer to collect data and measure the results of the management training program.

Agreeing on the follow-up is a crucial step in the transfer process. What you do *before* sending an employee to training is very important to the learning process.

To summarize step one in the process, before employees attend training, someone should spend a few minutes coaching and counseling them about the program. It serves to lower anxiety they have about training and clarifies reasons for sending them. It also provides an opportunity to answer their questions. If a manager is recommending several employees for the same program, coach and counsel them as a group. These are the concerns that need to be covered:

- Why they need training
- What is expected as a result
- How you will follow-up and evaluate

Step II—During Transition: Address Environmental Barriers

Environmental barriers are the problems that people encounter in their work environment. Trainees can overcome a few barriers in an attempt to apply new skills and ideas. However, if there are too many barriers, they will give up and decide it's not worth it; their work environment just won't support the change. It's important to the transfer process that barriers be kept to a minimum so trainees can bring back new ideas.

The second step in the transfer process is addressing barriers during transition. Transition occurs when employees return to work and try to assimilate their new skills and ideas into their environment. When employees first return to work they generally have all kinds of enthusiasm for the new ideas they want to try out. However, they often run into environmental barriers that prevent them from using what they were trained to do. The barriers can actually sabotage employees with good intentions. In this chapter, we will look at some typical environmental barriers employees face.

Some employees have no problem making the transition, others need some help. By evaluating the training and the trainee's progress you are able to discover barriers and do something to knock them down and pave the way for the employee. Many environmental barriers are things the employee has no power to fix. It takes a manager with clout to address these issues.

No Role Model. When an employee returns from training, there needs to be at least one role model who is doing things "right," the way they have been trained. Experienced employees frequently develop shortcuts, and the trainee returns to the work site to find that no one does it "the way it should be done." They will soon forget what was learned in training and do what the others are doing.

If the manager is not in a position to serve as a role model, look around for someone who can set a good example. For instance, tell employees when they return to "Watch Sally, she does it the way I want you to do it." When employees are on the job, they quickly pick up what peers do and forget what they learned in training.

> *Example*: A new employee for a chain of travel agencies was sent to a training program to learn how to fill out tickets and forms. She wrote large group cruise business. There were long forms to fill out for each group. She learned the correct way in training but when she started working, she found that the other agents skipped several pages of the forms. This saved them a lot of time. Besides, the forms were long, boring and repetitive. She found that by turning in the incomplete forms, she would get a phone call from the main office and the staff there would complain, but they would complete the forms. Guess how her forms were turned in, even though she knew the correct way?

This was not a matter of retraining, even though it would appear, at first glance, that she didn't know how to fill out the forms properly. The manager was not even aware that this was occurring until the home office asked him to evaluate the new agent's training. It was then that he discovered all his agents were able to complete the forms correctly, but simply did what the others did, which put a burden on the home office staff instead of on them. So ==consider what kinds of role models your new trainees have in their environment.==

Nonconducive Work Environment. Occasionally, trainees return to the work site to find their work stations or the room setup prevents them from doing what they were trained to do. The company, the managers, and the trainees would like to comply with company policy, but the environment interferes with their efforts. The trainee does not have the authority to change the work area. But you might be able to direct the problem to the proper person. Sometimes it's a small detail that managers might not realize is the root of a problem.

> *Example*: A chain of copy shops wanted to focus on quick, efficient customer service. It was important to customers that their work be ready on time and, most of all, that their precious work was well cared for. The policy and training reflected those needs. As soon as a customer walked up to the counter with a receipt to retrieve their order, the employee was to take it from a nearby shelf and hand it to the cashier. The problem was the lack of room on the "nearby" shelf. Orders were piled on top of one another and often a customer would be handed not only his, but a part of someone else's. Employees spent time trying to find orders that were not on the "nearby" shelf and put somewhere else by someone who was not there that day. Customers complained about poor service. Employees complained about other employees. The regional manager was asked to evaluate the training program in several shops to find out why things were not going smoothly. He assumed employees were not following training procedures when he discovered this work setup problem. The regional manager ordered new shelves built to accommodate the business, with plenty of room to separate and label each order.

In an attempt to evaluate training, the manager found an environmental barrier that prevented well-trained and well-meaning employees from doing their jobs. In fact, proper training was causing stress for the employees. It showed them how things could be and should be with a conducive work environment. This made their own lack of space even more frustrating.

No Opportunity to Practice. When employees return from training, they need an opportunity to practice what they have learned or they will *soon* forget it. It is up to the managers to provide those opportunities. If, in fact, employees do not need to use that skill on the job, why waste time and money teaching them how to do it? Training programs for people should be tailored to teach the skills employees actually use. Occasionally, employees learn additional things that are nice to know but not relevant in their department. Evaluate employees on objectives you have coached them to bring back, then give them a chance to practice those skills.

> *Example*: A secretary went to training to learn how to use some new software for computing monthly budgets. She progressed nicely in the class, but it was important for her to practice to really learn it and feel comfortable enough to use it. When she returned to the work site, it was business as usual. Phones ringing, salespeople to deal with, reports to get out, and the typical daily crises with no quiet time to practice her new skill. She did not have a computer at home, so she was left with a feeling of frustration. By the time she had an opportunity to use the software for a monthly budget report, she had forgotten how and went back to the old way. Wasted time and money!

She will have to be retrained if her boss expects her to do the budget using the new system. If the manager was using an evaluation system to check on her progress, he would have discovered this environmental barrier and provided time for her to practice using the new software program. So when it actually came time to prepare the budget, she would be ready. In this case, the barrier could have been handled by having someone else cover her desk for an hour each day while she practiced, or by paying her overtime to come in an hour early until she felt comfortable with the program. She had no control over the situation; only the manager had the authority to change her schedule or authorize overtime. Evaluating training would have discovered this environmental barrier, which had an easy solution.

Too Much, Too Fast. The best way to learn is in small steps, with time to practice new skills, before learning other, perhaps more complicated steps. One way is to train in modules that allow employees to think about new ideas and try them out at their work sites, then come back to ask questions about what worked and what did not, before giving them something new. Sometimes this is not practical. When training is provided on a quarterly or yearly basis and trainees fly in from far and wide, it may be necessary to load them down with everything they need to know in one or two weeks and send them back to work with information overload. It is too much to digest and lots of it is lost. However, a manager can address this barrier by helping employees sequence their learning skills. He can help them figure out what is most important and needs to be learned first—and what can wait until later.

> *Example*: A telephone company decided to develop a program for new staff analysts. The company's problem was that these people were taken off the line and promoted to staff analyst positions. But they really didn't understand their new role. It took too much time for managers to train them individually; so a consultant was hired to develop a five-day program that would cover everything they needed to know in their new jobs. The program was provided in major regions, but trainees flew in from various locations. When they left, they had a two-inch thick notebook and heads swimming with information. When they returned to the work site, their initial reaction was panic and questions on where to begin. In addition, "where to begin" was different for each of them. They had no control over this process. If their managers knew how to evaluate training, if they coached and counseled them before they attended, if they had made an agreement on follow-up, then they would both know how to address this barrier. The manager who sent the employees would sit down and help them sort out priorities. The manager would tell them which tasks were most important. The

manager would assign an easy task to begin with, and more difficult tasks as the employees' confidence increased. However, the manager would only discover the employee's plight and confusion as a result of evaluation. After all, the manager recommended training for role clarification.

Didn't Assign a Buddy. When employees return from training, it's hard for them to remember everything they learned—even with notes. Many trainees have a lot of pride, especially if they are technical or professional people with an education and a degree. They are reluctant to ask questions about things they think they should know. They do not want their manager to think they are stupid, that they can't remember, or didn't learn it well. Since this is very common, during this transition stage the new trainee may need a "buddy." The buddy is a peer who has been on the job and knows it well enough to answer questions and help the trainees before they get into a panic. The buddy is not an authority figure and has no power over the trainee. In other words, if the buddy thinks the trainees are stupid, it will not affect their future. If the boss thinks so, that's another matter.

> *Example*: A pharmaceutical lab technician is trained on several new procedures in class. One procedure was related to the proper temperature for storing petri dishes. Some needed refrigeration and others did not. In training, students are taught to label each dish immediately so they do not get confused. When they return to the lab, while concentrating on one thing, they occasionally forget something important. Because this is a pharmaceutical lab, one mistake can mean months of lost research time. A buddy who was assigned to work with the trainee during the transition was able to catch such a problem. The buddy merely kept an eye on the trainee and stepped in to help when needed. The buddy saw a petri dish with no label and impressed on the trainee the importance of this

oversight. The oversight would have affected the buddy's work as well as others in the lab. The buddy's job is to answer questions as well as catch costly mistakes.

The environmental barrier in this case might be the cultural norm to appear as if you know what you are doing; if you ask lots of questions, it's because you don't know. Another cultural norm is to say, "It's not my job to baby-sit the trainee." ==Assigning a buddy is one way you can help trainees overcome that barrier to help training transfer.==

No Benefit in Using the New Skill. Trainees need to see the value in using the new skill they are learning in a training class. Often it appears to them as more work without reason or reward. If the benefit of change isn't clearly defined, then there is not much chance of it occurring on the job, at least not with a willing attitude. Through evaluation, you are able to see if an employee is following company policy or a process. You or their manager can then step in to find out why not. It may require a little counseling to show the employee why it is done that way or how to work out a more acceptable way.

> *Example*: At a large telephone company, operators had been taught to respond to requests for information in a certain way. The procedure needed to be changed when deregulation allowed customers to use a different company for long distance calls. The operators needed a new response when a customer called using a competitor's credit card. Long distance operators were trained to respond with one message when people asked for assistance, but needed a different message if they were using a competitor's credit card. The operators found the new message long and difficult to work with. They wanted to say what they said previously because it was short and easy for them. The manager evaluated the training only to find some unhappy operators. He called a meeting with some trainees, staff people, and operators to work

out a new message that was acceptable to those who had to use it. They revised the message and retrained the operators.

This is how it should have been developed in the first place. Those who use it must see value in how it's done in order to fully cooperate. When the revised message was introduced, the results were good. The operators now understood the necessity for the new message and had some ownership in what was said.

Did Not Learn It Well. Some people learn faster than others and many will not try something unless they are sure they can do it well. This means employees may need to be retrained and retrained until they feel confident enough to change. This has to do with the rate at which people learn and their willingness to take risks.

Example: A company was promoting employee involvement by encouraging them to suggest improvements in their work areas. The employee suggestion system was well supported from top management down, and every employee was trained on the value of making suggestions and on the rewards they would receive. They were told how suggestions would be submitted, how a committee of peers would evaluate them, and how financial rewards would be dispersed. Employees were given forms for their first suggestion and told where to get additional forms. When the training was evaluated, the company was disappointed in the lack of forms turned in with suggestions for improvement. Certainly the managers heard complaints and ideas through the grapevine that could have been translated into profitable suggestions. During the evaluation process, an environmental barrier was discovered. Many of the workers were functionally illiterate or could not read and write in English. This prevented them from filling out the forms that required them to write a half-page description explaining their idea. After evaluating the training, this environmental barrier was addressed by allowing a bilingual clerk to spend some of her time helping employees put their ideas down on paper. She enjoyed this function and the workers liked discussing their ideas with someone who could help them with the wording.

Lack of Feedback. When employees return from training and try new skills, it's important to give them feedback on how well they are doing. They may think they understand what was taught in training, go off to the work site, and do the wrong thing very well. Someone needs to check their progress before new bad habits form.

Example: In a fast-food restaurant, trainees were sent to a training center, which was one store that was assigned to assist all the new people. It is a large store and open 24 hours a day. There are slow periods when the manager can work with the trainees during their transition period. They were given an orientation and introduced to operations in a classroom before they were assigned to the training center. Often when trainees start, a manager is eager to encourage them and allows certain mistakes to slip through the cracks while focusing on more important concerns. The problem is that bad habits can develop and then the trainee needs to unlearn and relearn. Wasted time and money! In the classroom, they were shown how to lift heavy objects without hurting their backs. During the evaluation process, the manager realized a trainee was not lifting correctly, even though the trainee thought he was. Feedback on the proper way was important before the trainee developed a bad habit, or worse, had a back injury and a workers compensation claim. Evaluation and timely feedback allowed the manager to catch this problem before it became a big problem.

Discouraged by Peers. The power of the peer group is very strong. Trainees may return from training, knowing very well what they are supposed to do and motivated to do well.

However, the environment they return to, with the norms established by the peer group, can affect the results of the program. Managers can often turn the problem around if they are aware of it. Sometimes they can't but at least the blame for the lack of productivity is placed properly on the environment and not on the training program.

> *Example*: A grocery distributor had an automated picking line that required workers to stack products on the line. The line could go as fast as workers could "pick" the product. A new, young, strong worker was trained to do the job. He came to work full of energy and determined to impress his boss. This was a union shop. At noon, a couple of older workers sidled up to him, poked him in the ribs, and said, "Slow down, kid. You're making us look bad. The union says we don't have to work that fast." Training was intended to improve speed and efficiency. By evaluating training to see why it hadn't increased productivity, this environmental barrier was uncovered. There are not many employees who are willing to ignore the pressure of the peer group.

Lack of Proper Equipment. This is a case of learning and unlearning. Frequently the equipment, tools, machines used in a training session are newer than the ones used on the job. Employees go to training, learn an operation on a machine or with a tool. They are familiar and comfortable with it as a result of training. When they return to the work site, they find something similar but different. It is a matter of unlearning and relearning. When employees go to training, the managers do not know, but generally assume, the equipment is the same. By evaluating the progress their employees are making, they might find out for the first time about the discrepancy.

Example: An employee in city government wants a promotion from file clerk to staff assistant. To qualify for promotion, she needs to be computer literate. She enrolls in a computer class at the local junior college, making sure they use IBM equipment. She finds they use an IBM compatible, which is not the same to her, but was the same to the person on the phone giving her information. The software they used was also "compatible," but not the same. Although she could now use computers, she was not familiar with the ones at work and did not score well on the test she needed for promotion. For this employee the junior college class was—wasted time and money!

There are all kinds of environmental barriers that can interfere with trainees when they return to work. By evaluating progress during the transition period, you might find some things that surprise you. Take a look at the work environment and talk to some employees. They may be more than willing to tell you what prevents them from doing on the job what they were trained to do in class. They may know a better way, the right way, but the environment is preventing them from doing their best. You need to help employees overcome environmental barriers if training is going to be **worth every penny.**

Step III—After Training: Reward and Reinforce

There needs to be a follow-up and reward for making the effort to improve. There must also be reinforcement to continue maintaining the gain. The improvements made in training will not continue without some attention. The third step in the transfer process is to reward and reinforce what was learned in the classroom when the trainee returns to work. There are many ways to follow-up training with rewards and reinforcement. Follow-up can take place right after training or several months down the road. Like the rest of the On-Target system, it's flexible. Rewards must be tailored for the situation. They must be part of a frame with a proper fit.

What motivates one employee may not motivate another. The system includes reward and reinforcement, but you have the flexibility to select appropriate ones based on the employees, their manager, and what your organization will allow. The only rule for rewards is that they must be *rewarding*. A reward for one employee may be a punishment for another.

- Howard, a shy accountant working for a large aerospace company, is an example. He found a huge error in their accounting system that cost the company close to a half million dollars. By adjusting the error and rebilling the client, they were able to recover the money. In an effort to reward Howard, his manager presented him with a check in front of the entire company at an awards banquet. His manager surprised Howard by calling him on stage, handing him the microphone and asking him to say a few words. Howard was so embarrassed he could not speak; in fact, he began to stutter. Howard would have preferred the check handed to him in private and a simple "atta boy" from his boss. Be sure you know your employee, and make the reward genuinely rewarding.

Once the new skill has become a habit, part of the culture, and the employee sees value in using it, you no longer need to pay as much attention to it. Occasionally, when someone slips back into old habits, it might require an extra dose of attention and reinforcement. Just to clarify the intent of rewards; good performance must always be recognized and reinforced, but extra attention and special rewards are needed to encourage change.

Some rewards can come from HRD. The most significant rewards come from the employee's supervisor. The best situation is when managers and HRD work together. Certificates of completion are often given at the end of training. They are more significant if they are presented by the manager along with a few pats on the back.

Get to know your people and what it takes to motivate them. What if you said to an employee, "We've made a significant investment in training you. What will it take to make this change stick?" You might be surprised at the answers you get.

Consider Your Options

If you were brainstorming on the possible rewards you or others could give for achieving training results, how many could you come up with? Many managers give rewards subtly with a compliment or a look of approval. Many make an effort to physically and publicly show recognition. Let's look at several options. See if they are methods you could use.

Performance Appraisal is one that almost everyone can use. If employees are in trouble, a warning notice shows up in their file and it is addressed at performance appraisal time. How often is an achievement remembered and mentioned at performance appraisal time? The On-Target Evaluation Chart could be used to coach and counsel before training, used to track environmental barriers during transition, and put in the employee's file after training. The employee would then be recognized for training at performance appraisal time. Most managers do not remember several months later at performance appraisal time that a particular employee has acquired a new skill or made an effort to improve. By using the evaluation chart, managers can have a reminder in the employee's file for each training program that was attended during the year. This is one of the most significant ways of rewarding and reinforcing training. Not only is it noticed; it provides validation for employees and a permanent record of their achievements. I strongly recommend that every time an investment is made in employee training, a reminder be filed so the manager and employee can tell if it was worthwhile months or years later.

Celebrations. There is a film used occasionally in training sessions called *Sand Castles*. It shows a supervisor working with his team to build this wonderful sand castle. Everyone works very hard and when the job is done, they all celebrate. There are many ways to celebrate achievements. You can take an individual out to lunch or for a beer after work. You can bring doughnuts or a box of candy to the office at the end of a training effort. There can be a formal celebration after training that led to meeting department goals.

How could you celebrate the completion of a training program with your trainees? Think of the individuals you work with. What would be significant to them? A staff that completed team training might want a party with others in the office included. A newly promoted manager who just completed three weeks of management training might want time alone with the boss in an elegant restaurant to discuss future goals and challenges. A group of new real estate agents that completed "new agent training" might prefer a festive, thrifty luncheon to rehash what was learned and how it can be applied most effectively. A conscientious, supportive secretary who took a new computer graphics program to improve presentations might respond more to a few pats on the back and a word about how much the new skill will help her manager and others in the department. Think about your employees and how they would want to celebrate success.

Awards. Giving someone a token of appreciation is a good way to reinforce or culminate a training effort; certificates of completion are meant to serve this purpose. Employees could be encouraged to frame their certificates or you could make copies to put in their personnel files. Because employees often ask if they will get a certificate at the end of a training program, we can safely assume the certificates must be significant to those employees.

Once I was training supervisors in a telephone company. Their employees were telephone pole climbers, the ones who splice wires and such. Their training is long, difficult, frequently in cold, wet weather, and possibly life-threatening. I jokingly said they should be rewarded with a pink rose when their training was finished. They laughed and booed and then, appropriately, started thinking of what might be a good reward for someone who completed this rigorous training. They decided the "guys" would like a jacket with the company logo on it as a symbol of achievement.

An award needs to be tangible. It is the type of thing you buy in a catalogue, like mugs, engraved pens, paper weights, card cases, etc. It can be simple and inexpensive or an expensive gift. A personal note from their manager or a formal letter on company stationery is the award most requested by employees. It is something they can show to others with pride. What could you give your employees as an award for completing training?

Recognition. This is an intangible reward, but just as significant to many people. Again, there are many ways to recognize people for their achievements. The key is that the recognition must be specific—better yet, specifically related to the training and the improved performance that resulted from training.

A friend trains people to arrange their offices to get the best use of space and how to manage files and paperwork. A client of hers who is a financial planner said that he not only had his most productive month, but the recognition he gets from peers who go "on and on" about his clean office is additional reinforcement.

Many organizations have an employee-of-the-month program that gives recognition for success. Their pictures are prominently displayed where friends and visitors can see them.

Some organizations use their newsletters for recognition. The newsletters recognize teams that solve problems, individuals who make suggestions that are used, and departments that reach goals.

As a trainer and outside consultant, I was overwhelmed by trainers who arranged a luncheon as recognition for the contribution the Total Quality program made to their organization. Their enthusiasm for the training was the best reward I could receive.

Employees like to be recognized in different ways. When you use the On-Target Evaluation System, you can discuss during the coaching and counseling stage how employees would like to be recognized for their successes before they are sent to training. It will not only serve as an incentive, it will provide insight to your employees and what is important to them.

Achieving Goals. For many employees, achieving goals is rewarding and reinforcing. For some self-motivated self-starters, simply setting a goal to strive for is all they need. They are self-disciplined enough to stay on track with very little pushing from anyone. They only need help in the beginning to realize what are realistic and possible goals. Other people need lots of reinforcing and very small steps to achieve when heading for a goal. These employees will require more time; in fact, your time or their manager's time is their reward, not the goal itself. The goal provides an opportunity to get frequent pats on the back and appreciation for their progress and effort to change.

Some people see a goal as a challenge or a stepping stone to more lofty objectives such as their boss's job, which is fine because they can then move up.

Accomplishing a goal may be linked with another reward, celebration, or recognition to culminate the achievement. But for many employees, achieving the goal is reward enough. They only need a self-assessment checklist or something to help them keep track of their progress. Their reward is in the process, the challenge of achieving the goal. The key is to have clear, measurable and achievable goals.

Feedback. Frequent feedback is the most overlooked and underused management tool. People want to be included in the information loop, they want to know what is happening, particularly as it pertains to them and their progress. Without feedback, employees get information using their own devices. The grapevine and their own wild imaginations take over. Direct feedback on how they are doing is a reward and reinforcer. It is even a reward when the news is not good, because what they imagine is often worse.

There are many ways you can give feedback as it relates to training. If it's training on a company-wide program, send memos on progress and productivity to everyone involved. If it's training for a department, give feedback at a staff meeting and let them ask questions. If it is a training session for individuals to improve knowledge, skill, or attitude, give them personal feedback on how you think they are doing. The evaluation process will help you identify environmental barriers, and so will feedback sessions between you and the employee. Feedback from their manager is equally important. Managers need to be coached on the importance of feedback and how to give it. Do not underestimate the power of non-verbal feedback. A look or a gesture can often tell more than words. Use non-verbal messages to convey approval to employees. A pat on the back, a wink, a nod of the head, can frequently convey your approval more than words.

Is it a "Catch 22"? The one thing employees want more of is feedback from their bosses on how they are doing. The form it comes in is not important. It can be written, spoken, or non-verbal. It can be formal or informal. What's important to employees is that they are clear about how they are doing. They would rather have bad news and fix the problem than not know and continue to do it wrong. When employees describe a good boss, it generally includes a comment on constructive feedback such as, "He lets me know how I'm doing." One thing managers like the least is giving personal feedback to employees on how they are doing. I think this is because managers interpret feedback as a formal discussion involving problems, instead of expanding to the many ways they are able to convey messages to employees and each other. I have rarely heard employees say their boss gave them too much feedback or communicated with them too often.

Team Effort. Instead of providing environmental barriers, the rest of the staff can rally to help trainees learn and use their new skills. They can, as a group, reward and reinforce training. It is the job of the manager to encourage them to do so. Encouragement from peers can be a significant stimulant to acquire new skills. The rewards they provide may not be tangible or in the form of celebration; however, their approval or disapproval can be powerful.

Last Resort—Lack of Punishment. Lack of punishment is a reward. Keeping one's job can be the best reward and greatest incentive. This is often the case when an employee needs to be retrained because his job function or department has been eliminated. Then the training is linked to lack of punishment, which would be "no job" if they are not retrained. Their reward is another position.

Need More Ideas? Ask your employees. Either as individuals or at a staff meeting. You might expect they will ask for the sky. Just the opposite is usually true. When I have done this in training sessions as a brainstorming activity, they come up with wonderful, simple, creative ideas management would never think of as a reward. Most of the ideas are realistic, possible and practical.

To summarize, reward and reinforcement is the third crucial part of the process in making training transfer from the classroom to the work site. Michael LeBoeuf, author of *The Greatest Management Principle in the World*, says, "What gets rewarded gets done." If employees are to maintain the gains made in training, they must know what's in it for them. What is their reward for improving their performance—an improvement that will heighten productivity?

The good news is that you have all kinds of rewards at your disposal. You need to stretch your imagination regarding creative possibilities and ask employees what they consider rewarding. They will tell you the rewards that make training an incentive.

Chapter 7. How Managers Use the Process

The On-Target Evaluation Chart is a tool to guide you through the three-step process:

- For coaching and counseling before training, it helps determine a follow-up method and establishes agreement between managers and trainees. It provides a record of whom went to which training program.
- By evaluating training during transition, it helps identify environmental barriers. It gives you a system to record the progress of each employee and assist those who need help.
- After training, the chart shows those who have made progress and need to be rewarded as well as those who need reinforcement. At performance appraisal time, managers have a reminder to give credit to those who have improved.

Let's look at our three managers, Samantha, Pete and Harry, to see how they could use the evaluation process with their employees. Each of these managers is sending an employee to training for a different reason. Each manager has a different management style. Each program is different. We need different methods of evaluation for each situation, a different frame for each picture. Yet the *before*, *during* and *after* process remains the same.

Samantha and Anne

Before Training: Samantha is our task-oriented manager who is concerned about getting the newsletter out on time. She wants Anne to become more competent on the computer and increase her speed.

When Samantha sends Anne to training, she spends some time coaching her to prepare her for the program. She explains that the newsletter is consistently late and that it needs to be on time. Samantha emphasizes that if Anne could increase her speed on the computer, make fewer errors, and learn to use mail merge, she thinks the newsletter would get out on time. Samantha continues coaching and counseling by explaining that she received a flyer on a computer class that seems to fill the bill. It will focus on the objectives and skills Anne needs, and provide work in small groups with one-on-one instruction when needed.

Samantha and Anne fill out the evaluation chart and together decide how they will follow-up and evaluate the results of the program. They decide to use a pretest/posttest by timing Anne's speed before she goes to training. They will time her again after training to see how much her speed increased. They agree it will take some time for Anne to practice before a significant improvement can occur. They feel there should be improvement in one month if Anne is given practice time. The posttest is scheduled for one month after training, and that date is written on the evaluation chart to remind both Samantha and Anne of their commitment.

Since Anne has not used mail merge before, they cannot use pretest/posttest. For this skill, Samantha will observe Anne practicing her new skill. In addition, she will count how many names can be merged and expect an increase as Anne's skill improves. They agree she should be able to demonstrate the merge system within a week after training, so they enter that date on the evaluation chart.

Samantha's final evaluation will be *results*. Does the newsletter get out on time? Samantha's goal is for it to be out on time within two months. She will use that document as the final test and enters the date on the evaluation chart.

Because Samantha is the type of manager who wants "proof," she is willing to invest a significant amount of time in Anne's progress. She has chosen evaluation methods that will give her numerical results to prove to her that Anne's training was worth the investment.

During Transition: Samantha will need to help Anne make the transition and ensure that her learning transfers from the classroom to the work site. Samantha can address in advance a few barriers Anne is likely to run into. First, she could provide an hour a day for Anne to practice her new skills. This could be done by having someone else cover Anne's desk during a slow period of the day, or by hiring a temporary, or by paying Anne overtime to come in early and use the computer. Samantha would take care to see that the mail merge software they use is the same Anne learned in class, so Anne doesn't have to unlearn and relearn. When Samantha evaluates Anne's progress on the agreed dates, she might find other barriers that have prevented Anne from accomplishing what they both expected. By evaluating the training, they'll uncover these barriers and Samantha and Anne can address them.

After Training: When Anne's transition is complete and the evaluation is finished, Samantha will have the data and the results she wants. She will be able to tell if Anne's speed has improved as a result of training by looking at the pretest/posttest times. She will know if Anne has, in fact, learned the mail merge system and how fast she inputs names. She will also have measurable results with a newsletter that is delivered on time. For her effort in accomplishing this goal, Anne must be rewarded.

- The time and money invested in Anne's training is a reward. It shows Anne that the company appreciates her potential and is willing to help her improve her skill rather than find someone else to do the newsletter.
- The time and attention Anne gets from Samantha is a reward that reinforces their working relationship. Most employees would like to have more time and attention from their supervisors.
- Verbal praise from Samantha as Anne's skill improves should not be underestimated as a way to reward and reinforce learning.
- When the newsletter comes out on time, Samantha and the others involved need to celebrate. A gesture of appreciation for a goal that is reached is all that is needed.

This is how Samantha and Anne could go through the evaluation process for their unique situation. The evaluation chart is used as a guide for both of them before training, during transition and after training. The final step is for Samantha to comment on the results of the training program on the evaluation chart. She might want to recommend more training or just comment on Anne's progress. The chart will go in Anne's file as a reminder for her performance appraisal. Samantha might want to make a note to herself on the training program in case she needs to send another employee to this training class. The chart is a tool, and the process is complete.

Pete and Lisa

Before Training: Pete is our practical manager who wants to prepare Lisa for a supervisory position. Pete coaches and counsels Lisa by discussing his future plans for her and his confidence in her ability to take on added responsibility. This lets Lisa know why she is being trained to do a job previously done by her supervisor. Pete explains that he wants her to learn to fix the new machinery as a back-up to the supervisor at first and eventually wants Lisa to take over the function. Pete describes the program he has in mind to teach her how to work with delicate equipment. Pete and Lisa collaborate to decide how they will follow-up and evaluate the training program and her progress.

Pete first wants to know if Lisa will like this new assignment and be willing to do this type of work. They agree to interview her immediately after the program to see if she is interested before assigning her to it. They put a date on the evaluation chart for the day after her program is complete. If she decides to go on, he will observe her handle the equipment to make sure she learned it correctly. Pete has a certain way he likes machines handled and needs to teach Lisa how to adapt what she learned in class to what is appropriate for his technicians. They agree to let Lisa work on one piece of equipment at a time, then check with him when she is ready to move on. They agree to have Lisa fill out an action plan, which will have a date for the observation, a date to review and fine tune the machines, and a date for Lisa to take over her new function. The action plan will be complete in one month. They will then be able to determine the results of training.

During Transition: While Lisa is being trained, Pete needs to anticipate environmental barriers. He might have to work with Lisa's supervisor to explain why he's training Lisa to do this job. During transition, Pete might need to assign a supervisor from another department to help Lisa if she has problems. Primarily, Pete will have to show Lisa he has confidence in her potential. If she can handle this new assignment, then future supervisory training programs might be in order. By evaluating the training, he will get a better perspective on Lisa as a future supervisor. He will also find out if he has to deal with other barriers such as problems with her peers and supervisor.

After Training: How can Pete reward and reinforce Lisa's progress?

- He could record and mention her new function at performance appraisal time, perhaps even change her job description.
- Pete could recommend Lisa for more supervisory training and recommend her when a supervisory position becomes available.
- Pete's confidence and mentoring of Lisa will provide reward and reinforcement.
- The challenge of learning new procedures provides personal gratification.
- Recognition of increased responsibility is a motivator and reward for competent employees.

The evaluation process is different for Pete and Lisa. It is suited to their unique situation. Pete, unlike Samantha, is not interested in collecting numerical data on her skills. He is interested in training a potential supervisor and seeing if she is suited for the new position. He is also interested in transferring a job function to her. If that works out as a result of training, it will increase his department's productivity and solve his staffing problems.

Harry and David

Before Training: Harry is our easy-going manager who's concerned about his salesman's recent slump. David, his number one salesman, is equally concerned. Harry and David also have a unique situation. David approached Harry about his sales slump. The request for training originated with the employee.

Harry found a seminar he hopes will help David out of his slump. Before training, Harry tells David about the seminar and the highly touted reputation of the instructor. There is no question about why Harry wants David to go or why David wants to attend. They have a common concern for David's loss of confidence, which is reflected in his sales.

Harry and David agree to evaluate the training in two ways. They will talk after the program to see if David feels more confident and inspired to try new techniques. They will also track David's sales records to see if he is more productive after training. On the evaluation chart they agree to an informal interview within a week after the program and to create a tracking chart for the next six months.

During Transition: David's transition will be the six months following training during which his sales are being tracked. During this time, he might run into outside barriers that affect sales. The market could change, the economy could be a factor, other barriers could affect David's sales. During this time, Harry will need to stay in touch to see how David is doing. David may need an extra dose of attention and a few "atta boys" to inspire him.

A salesman needs to be enthusiastic and confident. By losing his confidence, he could once again talk himself into a slump. He might need Harry's help immediately after the training program is over, until his sales bounce back.

After Training: The results from the sales seminar will be evaluated in two ways. First, Harry will stay in touch with David to keep a pulse on his self-confidence. Second, they will both pay attention to the tracking chart and not measure results until it is complete. The appropriate reward will be evident to both of them.

- For some employees, just the act of tracking their progress motivates them toward accomplishing a goal.
- David's sales commissions will probably increase and Harry's departmental productivity will also increase.
- An unintended outcome and reward might be David's faith in Harry as a supervisor. David may feel Harry cares about him and is willing to stick by him and help when he is down. He now feels Harry wouldn't say, "Make the numbers or leave."
- This situation calls for a reward that's personal between David and Harry in addition to bonus or commission—perhaps dinner together or a trip. The "I-bet-you" type of reward.

The evaluation process is different for David and Harry. Their unique situation required tracking numbers, but Harry's real concern was with motivation and renewed confidence. Their evaluation methods need to address both issues. Harry's comments on the evaluation chart could be about the quality of the seminar for future reference for other salesman or it could be about David to see if slumps are a recurring problem.

In summary, the *process* has three simple steps that are flexible based on the manager, the trainee and the situation.

- **First,** coach and counsel to prepare trainees for the program. Tell them why they need this training and why you are willing to spend the time and money on this program for them.
- **Second,** identify and address environmental barriers that can sabotage their enthusiasm and new skills.
- **Third**, reward and reinforce progress to make sure new skills will last. This process can help managers meet their goals and make the investment in training ***worth every penny.***

Chapter 8. Closing the Loop

There is one final step in the On-Target Evaluation System. Now that you have completed the three-step evaluation process, you have information about the training program that needs to be fed back to the managers and participants. You need to close the loop by making sure the programs that are provided are doing the job and those concerned receive the results from the data that was collected.

So far, we've assumed the training program itself was wonderful. That the program objectives, as stated, were actually covered in the classroom. That the trainees left the classroom knowing how to do the things they were sent to learn. We have assumed up to this point that the training program was based on department needs and the needs of the employees. We have also assumed department needs are driven by organizational goals. We have assumed if managers are doing their job in the evaluation process that training and HRD are doing their jobs. Your job means you've arranged for the following:

- *Coaching and counseling* employees before sending them to training so they know exactly what is expected of them and how performance will be evaluated.

- ***Addressing environmental barriers*** during transition so that trainees can use their new skills and ideas.
- ***Rewarding and reinforcing*** employees after training to ensure that the gain will be maintained and that they understand the benefits for changing.

Sometimes our assumptions are wrong! Sometimes the program is at fault, and employees are not getting what they need. At the bottom of the On-Target Evaluation Chart is a place for comments. This is designed to give you an opportunity to gather data for whomever provides training. You will be able to document what worked and what did not. After evaluating several employees, you are now in a position to be specific about how the program should be modified to better meet their needs. If you are not getting improved performance, perhaps it is a poorly designed program or a poor instructor.

Let's look at a couple of possibilities:

1. ***Faulty Program***: The program itself could be a loser. It could be poorly designed, too long, or not built on adult learning principles. It could be inappropriate for the level of the learners by giving them information they know or that's over their heads. Perhaps it provides some of the information the trainees need, but not enough. The manager needs to provide evaluation data, after sending several people, so that the course can be modified. To make changes and improve, HRD needs feedback from evaluation on the quality of the program.

2. ***Poor Instructor***: There are many organizations that purchase off-the-shelf programs and have managers take turns teaching them. Some managers have a flair for instruction and do a great job. Others do not, and the students suffer. One company I know of feels that being a trainer is good for a manager's development. It gives them visibility, teaches them presentation skills and is a step on their ladder to success. Unfortunately, their

students feel like guinea pigs. They resist going to any training programs because it's luck of the draw as to whether they got a good instructor that day or a terrible one.

3. ***Faulty Objectives***: Frequently, programs initiated by corporate headquarters and provided for employees in other locations miss their mark. The managers who intend to send participants must validate the program's goals. That way, headquarters will design a program based on their needs.

There are other things that can cause the program itself to fall short of its potential. However, far too often managers are anxious to point a finger at the program instead of facing their own responsibility in supporting training.

If Samantha, Pete and Harry were making comments on their employees, they might read as follows:

> ***Samantha***: "Anne's training on computer skills improved her speed by 20 words per minute as demonstrated by her pretest/posttest times. She has demonstrated an ability to use the mail merge, and her skill is 70% accurate after training. In three months, that percent should increase to 95% with practice. We delivered the newsletter on time this month."

These comments are for Samantha's use about Anne's progress, and to help her see if the training program met her needs. If Anne had not done well, Samantha could check with the instructor to see if Anne was different than the other students. Perhaps Anne slept through the program or made no effort to learn. Samantha could also check with other managers to see how their employees fared in the same program. Perhaps there was a new instructor or another problem with the program.

> ***Pete***: "Lisa enjoyed the program and is interested in the task as it was taught. She has successfully fixed several delicate machines; however, each time I send employees to learn how to adjust machinery, I need to retrain them. I would like to meet with trainers to show them how I want my technicians trained."

These comments are intended for HRD people to help them modify or improve their program to meet Pete's needs. After evaluating several trainees, there are specific suggestions he can make to help the training department meet his needs.

> ***Harry***: "David is doing much better after attending the XYZ Sales Training Program. The program helped David rebuild his confidence and improve sales. I would recommend it for salesmen in similar situations. David raved about the instructor, the quality of the program, and the impact it had on him."

These comments are directed at David. They let him know Harry is pleased with his progress. They are also notes for Harry to remind him about the program's quality. It will remind him of a method to inspire David and others in similar slumps.

The evaluation process provides a way to make sure that you, and managers, are doing your part. Comments on the On-Target Evaluation Chart provide opportunities for managers to communicate with those who provide training. It's important that training be designed to meet their needs. And it's important that managers have a method to give specific feedback, with evaluation data, to the training department about what their needs are. By evaluating the results of training, you'll have that information.

Chapter 9. Putting It All Together

Evaluation is a tool to help you get value out of the investment in training. It is used to get learning to transfer from the classroom to the work site.

Why Evaluate Training?

Why do *you* want to evaluate training? What do *you* need to know about the training provided for your employees? This information should be your reason for evaluating the results. The other reason is that someone else, such as your boss, is asking you to justify your training budget. Even if you don't care, you need to provide the data.

Here are some reasons you might have to follow-up training with evaluation:

- Your boss asks for data.
- You believe that if trainees know there will be a follow-up, they will enter training with better attitudes.
- The coaching and counseling develops a better rapport between managers and employees.
- It clarifies changes expected as a result of training.

- Evaluation gives training credibility.
- Evaluation helps you discover environmental barriers, reasons why trainees are not improving even though they have been trained.
- It provides a tracking system of who went where and, with the evaluation chart, a document for employee files.
- Evaluation provides a basis for rewards and reinforcement. Employees love to celebrate their achievements.
- It provides a way for managers to communicate with those who provide training, so they can design training to meet their needs.

Don't evaluate training without a reason and way to *use* the information. Evaluation is a tool to help you accomplish something. There is no value in just collecting data. Too many evaluation reports end up on a shelf collecting dust. Know up front how the evaluation data will be used to make changes in the organization.

What Methods Can You Use?

What methods can you use to evaluate training? You can use any method that works for you—any method at all that gives you the information you need. There is no one right way to evaluate training. It's simply a tool to help you answer your questions about training. I have dozens of methods for evaluation in my files. Some are very creative, some are so obvious they tend to be overlooked and some are so complicated they hardly seem worth the effort.

These are the ones I've found most practical and should cover most training needs.

- ***Interviews.*** Talk to people, they will tell you what you need to know—sometimes a lot more than you expected.
- ***Questionnaires.*** Survey people. You can cover a lot of territory and the responses can be anonymous.

- ***Observations.*** Look for results. How do you want to see people perform? A checklist can help you be objective.
- ***Action Plans.*** Let your employees decide what changes they will make; you offer support.
- ***Tracking Charts.*** Make it a game. Keep track of the department goals, team or individual progress with a chart or graph.

How to Choose an Instrument

How do I choose an evaluation instrument? Link evaluation to your needs assessment and program objectives.

- ***Needs Assessment.*** Why was this training program offered in the first place? Customer complaints, grievances from the rank and file, or mandate from higher authority? Go to the source to collect information on results.
- ***Program Objectives.*** What are you trying to accomplish in this three-hour or three-week program. Look at what trainees are actually learning in the program to evaluate results.
- ***Evaluation.*** Use the On-Target Evaluation Chart. It will help you consider your options. Combine a data source with a method for collecting information. There are generally several options that will work. Your choice of an evaluation instrument is not that important, as long as it gives you the information you want and it is documented consistently.

Three-Step Process

What is the three-step evaluation process? The process is much more important than the instrument you use. Almost any evaluation instrument will do. The process, however, is what leads to the transfer of learning, which is our reason for evaluating training.

Before Training—Coach and Counsel

- Explain why training is recommended for the employee.
- Tell them what they are expected to learn and bring back to their department.
- Collaborate on a method for follow-up. Let them know the program has support and that achieving results is important enough to follow-up.

During Transition—Address Environmental Barriers

There probably will be barriers your trainees will run into when they return to work and try new skills. Your organization might provide some unique barriers. It's your job to help managers identify and address barriers before they sabotage the enthusiasm and progress made in training.

After Training—Reward and Reinforce

If the gain is to be maintained, it must be reinforced and rewarded. Evaluation will help you establish a policy to reinforce what was learned in training—you can periodically review and give extra assistance to those needing it. Evaluation will also give you a criterion for celebrating success. Even a token, such as a certificate of completion, is meaningful to employees. If training improves performance and performance improves productivity, it calls for a celebration.

Working with Your Managers

How to work with HRD to make training better. HRD, the training people, can help by designing and providing evaluation instruments for managers. They can help tally and analyze the data and graphically depict results. But managers are the ones who need to provide the information. They are the only ones who really knows if an employee's performance has improved as a result of training. It is extremely important for management and HRD to work together as partners to provide training that meets these criteria.

- Training needs to support organizational goals as well as department goals.
- Training must meet managers' needs by improving the performance of their employees. Managers must convey their needs to HRD.
- Training must meet the employees' needs by helping them develop personally and professionally. Evaluation will help uncover their needs.

Final Words

Evaluation is simply a tool to help improve employees' performance and improve productivity. With your help, training can be much better. For the "care and feeding" of your employees, as well as for departmental productivity, training is *your* business. By attending to the simple three-step process, you and your managers can make a difference. You can make training in your organization ***worth every penny.***

A Note from the Author

To stay informed on future developments in training evaluation and training services, indicate your special interests below, clip this page and mail it to:

Jane Holcomb, Ph.D.
7805 W. 80th Street
Playa del Rey, CA 90291
Telephone: (310) 821-7624

I am interested in (check one or more):

❏ Seminars, workshops and lectures on training evaluation.

❏ Customized evaluation systems for your organization.

❏ Video— *Worth Every Penny*. How to use evaluation of training to promote the transfer of learning. Comes with Leaders Guide for Trainers. $200 (Previews are available for $100, which will be applied to purchase price.)

❏ Customized, three-hour *On-Target Training* modules for management development and customer service to meet the needs of trainees— with an evaluation component built in.

❏ Total quality training programs for service organizations individually designed and developed for your organization. Combining customer service and the total quality philosophy of service.

❏ Additional copies of this book including bulk sales at quantity discounts.

Name _____ Title _____

Company _____

Address _____

City _____ State _____ Zip _____

Telephone Number (___) _____